LET'S EXPLORE
inside the Bible

Fiona Walton

Illustration:
Tony Morris and Linda Kelsey

Scripture Union
130 City Road, London EC1V 2NJ.

Text: Fiona Walton
Illustration: Tony Morris and Linda Kelsey
Design: Liz Murphy
Cover Design: Ross Advertising
Editor: Elrose Hunter

© Scripture Union 1994
First published 1994
ISBN 0 86201 905 2

Printed and bound in Singapore.

Let's explore inside the Bible

Inside the Bible

It is always exciting to look inside things! It is fun to unwrap a parcel and find the gift inside. It is interesting to open the bonnet of a car and look at the different parts of the engine that make the car go. It is great to receive an envelope through the post and read its contents. It would be wonderful to discover valuable treasure! Even dogs like to look inside holes in the hope of finding bones!

It is exciting to look inside the Bible too! The Bible stories begin in the Stone Age, and over 2000 years later the Bible ends with stories of people in the Roman Empire!

People over the centuries have been prepared to die for the sake of the Bible's message and others have suffered in order to get a copy of it. Millions of people all over the world read the Bible each day!

Let's explore INSIDE THE BIBLE . . . .

How the Bible

The Bible is a collection of books divided into two sections - the **Old Testament** and the **New Testament.** There are thirty-nine books in the Old Testament and twenty-seven in the New Testament.

Can you work out how many books there are in the whole Bible?

These books were written by about thirty-five different authors over a period of at least fifteen hundred years. We don't know the names of all the writers, but we know that they all believed in God and listened to him. The Bible is God's message for people through the ages.

```
וְהָאָ֫רֶץ וְאֵת הַשָּׁמַ֫יִם
מְרַחֶ֫פֶת אֱלֹהִים וְר֫וּחַ תְה֫וֹם י
וַיַּ֫רְא וַֽיְהִי־א֫וֹר א֫וֹר יְהִ֫י ם
וּבֵ֫ין הָא֫וֹר בֵּ֫ין אֱלֹהִים כִּ֫י־ט֫וֹב
וַֽיְהִי־ קָרָ֫א לַלַּ֫יְלָה וְלַח֫שֶׁךְ י֫וֹם
פ
מַ֫יִם בֵּ֫ין מַבְדִּ֫יל וִיהִ֫י הַמַּ֫יִם ד
אֲשֶׁ֫ר הַמַּ֫יִם בֵּ֫ין וַיַּבְדֵּ֫ל קִ֫יעַ
וַֽיְהִי־כֵ֫ן לָרָקִ֫יעַ מֵעַ֫ל וַשֶׁ֫ר
י֫וֹם בֹּ֫קֶר וַֽיְהִי־ עֶ֫רֶב וַֽיְהִי־ ז
פ
אֶחָ֫ד אֶל־מָק֫וֹם הַשָּׁמַ֫יִם חַת
הָאָ֫רֶץ לַיַּבָּשָׁ֫ה אֱלֹהִים רָ֫א
```

LANGUAGES

The Old Testament

The books of the Old Testament were first written down in Hebrew, with a few pages in Aramaic. These were the ancient languages of the Jews.

On the left is part of the first page of a Hebrew Old Testament. Isn't it difficult to read!

It reads from right to left. Here is a sentence 'Praise the Lord' in Hebrew.

הַ֫לְל֫וּ - יָ֫ה

It is said . . .   *Hallel-ou-jah*

Have a go at copying it down.

Until 1947 the oldest known Hebrew manuscripts of the Old Testament dated from the ninth and tenth centuries. But in 1947 manuscripts a thousand years older were discovered by the Dead Sea. A shepherd boy happened to find old leather scrolls in pottery jars in a cave. He did not know that these were valuable, but archaeologists realised that they included copies of all the Old Testament books except Esther. The Dead Sea Scrolls belonged to a group of Jews who lived at Qumran near the Dead Sea. The Hebrew written down in the Bible is different from modern Hebrew spoken in the world today.

The New Testament

The New Testament was originally written down in Greek. On the right is part of the first page of a Greek New Testament. Here is the sentence 'Praise the Lord' in Greek.

Αἰνεῖτε τὸν Κύριον

It is said . . . .   *Ainyeete ton Kurion*

Now you can say 'Praise the Lord' in two languages besides your own! Have a go at learning it and copying it down.

There are thousands of early Greek manuscripts for scholars to look at, but nobody has seen the first texts that the Bible authors wrote themselves. There are also early translations of the New Testament in Latin, Egyptian, and other languages. The Greek written down in the Bible is different to the modern Greek spoken in the world today.

```
ΒΙΒΛΟΣ γενέσεως Ἰησοῦ
υἱοῦ Ἀβρααμ.
    Ἀβρααμ ἐγέννησεν τὸν Ἰ
νησεν τὸν Ιακωβ, Ιακωβ δὲ
καὶ τοὺς ἀδελφοὺς αὐτοῦ,
τὸν Φαρες καὶ τὸν Ζαρα ἐκ
ἐγέννησεν τὸν Εσρωμ, Εσρ
Αραμ, | Αραμ δὲ ἐγέννησεν
ναδαβ δὲ ἐγέννησεν τὸν Να
ἐγέννησεν τὸν Σαλμων, Σ
τὸν Βοες ἐκ τῆς Ραχαβ, Β
Ιωβηδ ἐκ τῆς Ρουθ, Ιωβ
Ιεσσαι, Ιεσσαι δὲ ἐγέννησεν
λέα. Δαυειδ δὲ ἐγέννησεν
τοῦ Οὐρίου, Σολομὼν δὲ ἐ
Ροβοαμ δὲ ἐγέννησεν τὸν Α
σεν τὸν Ασαφ, Ασαφ δὲ ἐγε
```

came to us

WRITING SURFACES AND WRITING TOOLS

People have been able to write for thousands of years, but they didn't always use pen and paper.

Can you make a list of things that can be used for writing with and on, besides pen and paper?

People in ancient times wrote or carved on stone, rock or on the walls of caves. Later clay tablets were used and victories in battles were recorded on monuments. By 1500 BC writing boards were in use. The board had a hollow which was filled with wax. A sharp pointed instrument was used for writing on the wax.

Notes were scratched on pieces of broken pottery. Lots of pieces of pottery have been found with letters, notes and bills written on them.

Thousands of years ago the Egyptians discovered that they could make a type of paper from papyrus reeds that grew around the river Nile. Sheets of papyrus were joined together and rolled up into a scroll. Scrolls could also be made of leather or parchment. Writing on papyrus or parchment was done with a reed pen, which was like a brush. This was later replaced by a quill pen. Ink was made from charcoal mixed with oil and a sticky kind of gum.

Printing wasn't invented until the fifteenth century and so all writing had to be hand copied. Scribes made copies of the Old and New Testament. They carefully checked their work against the original. Later, groups of scribes worked at the same time. The chief scribe read aloud the manuscript and the other scribes wrote it down.

Ask a friend to read five sentences from a book out loud. Write them down as you hear them.

Check whether you made any mistakes. Imagine what it would be like if you were writing large amounts for several hours.

MAKE A MINIATURE SCROLL

You will need: two cotton wool buds, a length of brown paper (an old envelope will do!), scissors, paste, thread, a dark brown or black felt tip pen.

1. Colour the two cotton buds black.
2. Then paste one to either end of the brown paper.
3. Use the brown pen to write the words of the verse from Scripture. Scripture means the Bible.

All Scripture is inspired by God.
2 Timothy 3:16

HOW WAS THE BIBLE COLLECTED?

The Old Testament

It is not known when the books of the Old Testament were collected together. The Jews believe that Ezra the scribe collected and arranged the books. Parts of most of the Old Testament books are quoted somewhere in the New Testament, so it seems that the thirty-nine books of our Old Testament were established by the time of Jesus. We know that one day Jesus read aloud in the synagogue in Nazareth from the book of Isaiah. You can read about it in the gospel of **Luke, chapter 4 verses 16-20.**

The New Testament

The followers of Jesus met together and heard readings from the Old Testament. But as they were worshipping Jesus it was important to have an account of Jesus' life and teaching. This was written down in the gospels so that people would be able to read them when the first disciples, who had been with Jesus, died. Letters written by Paul and others were read aloud to groups of Christians because they gave advice about living as a Christian. The accounts of Jesus' life and the letters of the early churches make up the New Testament that we know today.

HOW THE BIBLE CAME TO US

Our Bible is the result of many translations over hundreds of years. The first translations of parts of the Bible into Old English were done around AD 700. The first translation of the whole Bible into English was made by John Wycliffe in 1384. This was a hand-written translation from Latin. The first printed Bibles appeared in 1526.

There have been many new translations in English since then, especially in the twentieth century. The Bible has been translated into more than a thousand languages and translation is still continuing into languages spoken by small groups of people across the world.

How the Bible

THE BIBLE AS A LIBRARY

Have you ever visited a library or a bookshop? There are all sorts of different books on display. There are poetry books, stories, biographies, history books and books full of facts.
Can you think of any other types of writing?
The Bible is like a library or a bookshop. It contains a lot of different types of books.
Can you remember how many books there are in the Bible?
There are five types of books in the Bible.

1. HISTORY BOOKS

Perhaps you have history books at home or at school. **Can you think of a history book you have read?** History books contain facts and information about true events and real people. The Bible contains many history books.

Building with Bricks

Nehemiah is one of the history books in the Old Testament. The book of Nehemiah starts off with these words -
"This is the account of what Nehemiah son of Hacaliah accomplished. In the month of Kislev in the twentieth year that Artaxerxes was emperor of Persia, I, Nehemiah, was in Susa, the capital city."
(Nehemiah 1 v1)
The book goes on to tell how Nehemiah was made governor of Judea and how he returned to Jerusalem and inspired the people to rebuild the city walls which had been destroyed by invaders.

2. BOOKS OF LAWS

What are the rules in your school? What are the rules and laws in your country?
God gave laws to his people to live their lives by and to explain how they should worship him. Many of these laws are written down in the Bible.

Living Laws

The best known laws are the Ten Commandments which God gave to Moses to pass on to the people.
1. Worship no God but me.
2. Do not make for yourselves images of anything in heaven or on earth or in the water under the earth.
3. Do not use my name for evil purposes.
4. Observe the Sabbath and keep it holy.
5. Respect your father and mother.
6. Do not commit murder.
7. Do not commit adultery.
8. Do not steal.
9. Do not accuse anyone falsely.
10. Do not desire anything that someone else owns.
(Exodus 20 v3-4, 7-8, 12-17)

3. BOOKS OF PROPHECY

Prophets were God's messengers. Some of the messages they gave are written down in the Bible.

Bethlehem's Baby

Micah was a prophet who lived about seven hundred years before Jesus. The book of Micah is a collection of God's messages which Micah delivered to the people of Judah. Micah gave this message to the people, 'The Lord says, "Bethlehem, you are one of the smallest towns in Judah, but out of you I will bring a ruler for Israel, whose family line goes back to ancient times."'
(Micah 5 v2)
When do you think Micah's message came true? Who was born in Bethlehem?

4. POETRY BOOKS

Do you have a favourite poem? The Old Testament has books of poems and books of wise sayings.

Psalm Praise

There are 150 poems, songs and prayers in the book of Psalms which became the Jews' hymnbook and was used for worship.

Christians still use it when they are praising God.

Do you know some sad songs, poems or prayers?

Do you know some happy songs, poems or prayers?

The book of psalms has sad psalms, happy psalms, hopeful psalms and psalms that say sorry to God.

"I will praise you, Lord, with all my heart, I will tell of all the wonderful things you have done." (Psalm 9 v1)

"How much longer will you forget me, Lord? For ever? How much longer will you hide yourself from me?" (Psalm 13 v1)

"I have sinned against you - only against you - and done what you consider evil." (Psalm 51 v4)

5. BOOKS OF LETTERS

Do you enjoy getting a letter through the post? Have you ever kept a special letter? The New Testament contains many letters that were written to churches or individuals. The writers explain how to live as a Christian, they taught people about God and they tried to answer questions. The letters were kept and read in Christian services. Many of the letters were written by Paul.

Paul to Philemon

Paul wrote to Philemon, who was the leader of the church in Colossae. Onesimus, one of his slaves, had run away and met Paul. Onesimus had become a Christian. Paul sent him back to Philemon with a special letter. This is how Paul starts his letter, "From Paul, a prisoner for the sake of Christ Jesus, and from our brother Timothy to our friend and fellow-worker Philemon." (Philemon v1)

This is how Paul wrote about Onesimus, "If you think of me as your partner, welcome him back just as you would welcome me."

BIBLE BOOKS

THE APOCRYPHA

A number of other books known as the apocrypha or 'hidden books' are included in the Old Testament part of the Bibles used by the Roman Catholic and Greek Orthodox churches. They include history books, stories and wisdom literature.

POETRY BOOKS
Job
Psalms
Proverbs
• Ecclesiastes
Song of Songs

BOOKS OF LAWS
Genesis
Exodus
Leviticus
Numbers
Deuteronomy

HISTORY BOOKS
(Old Testament)
Joshua
Judges
Ruth
1 & 2 Samuel
1 & 2 Kings
1 & 2 Chronicles
Ezra
Nehemiah
Esther

(New Testament)
Matthew
Mark
Luke
John
Acts

BOOKS OF LETTERS
Romans
1 & 2 Corinthians
Galatians
Ephesians
Philippians
Colossians
1 & 2 Thessalonians
1 & 2 Timothy
Titus
Philemon
Hebrews
James
1 & 2 Peter
1,2 & 3 John
Jude

BOOKS OF PROPHECY
(Old Testament)
Isaiah
Jeremiah
Lamentations
Ezekiel
Daniel
Hosea
Joel
Amos
Obadiah
Jonah
Micah
Nahum
Habakkuk
Zephaniah
Haggai
Zechariah
Malachi

(New Testament)
Revelation

Camping in

CLOTHES IN CANAAN

The main materials used for making clothes were animal skins, goats' hair, sheep's wool and linen. The people liked to dye the material and embroider their clothes.

A picture painted on a tomb by an Egyptian artist shows us what Abraham and Sarah would probably have worn.

A man wore only a loin cloth or short skirt when he was working. At other times he might wear a tunic or shirt. Women wore tunics which came down to their ankles. Poor people had few clothes and had to look after them, but a rich person might have clothes for many different occasions.

Abraham was born in the city of Ur in the land of Mesopotamia. When he grew up, his family moved to the city of Haran and settled there. Abraham was wealthy and he and his wife Sarah had a comfortable home. But they had no children and this was a great sadness to them.

When Abraham reached the age of seventy-five he expected to spend his old age in Haran but God had other plans.

One day, God said to Abraham, 'I want you to pack up and leave this country and go to a new land that I am going to show you. I will bless you and give you as many descendants as the stars in the sky or the sand on the seashore. I will make your name famous and you will be a blessing to other people.'

Abraham trusted God and so he packed and went. He left his home in the city and set out with Sarah, his nephew Lot, his

A CIVILISED CITY

Ur was already an ancient city by the time Abraham was born there around 2000 BC.

Archaeologists have been digging up the old city. They have found the gold and silver treasures of local kings who lived about 400 years before Abraham! They have found baked clay tablets covered with writing. Some are records of sales between merchants and traders from faraway places. Others tell of family life in Ur. Well built houses with drains, schools and a large temple or ziggurat have been discovered.

Canaan

THE GOOD
NEWS IS ...
God had a plan for
Abraham's life. He has a plan
for everyone's life! We can trust
God to be with us, as he was
with Abraham.

servants, cattle and all his possessions. He had no idea where he was going, but he believed that God would show him the way. He knew God had a plan!

Abraham and his family lived in tents as they journeyed, camping wherever they found water. They moved slowly from place to place, finally arriving in the country of Canaan. There Abraham set up camp at Shechem, under a great oak tree. It was here that God told Abraham, 'Canaan is the new land I promised I would take you to. I am going to give this land to your descendants.'

Although they were both old, some years later Abraham and Sarah had a son, named Isaac.

Abraham trusted God and God kept his promise.

Find this story in the Bible in Genesis 11 v27-32 and 12 v1-9.

HOUSES OF HAIR

Abraham's tent was probably made of cloth woven from goats' hair. It was waterproof and kept out the heat. There were about nine tent poles, arranged in a rectangle. The goats' hair cloth was placed over the poles and fastened down with ropes and tent pegs. Each tent had two rooms, one for the men and the other for the women, the children and for cooking in. Women in rich families sometimes had their own tent, as Abraham's wife, Sarah, did.

Everything in the tent had to be carried by the donkeys, so there was little furniture and very few belongings. People sat and slept on mats. Cooking pots and clothes were hung from hooks on the tent poles.

FATHER OF A FAMILY

In Old Testament times family did not just mean a father, a mother, and their children. A family included parents, children, grandparents, aunts, uncles, cousins, nephews, nieces and even servants. A family could be very large!

ABRAHAM'S TRAVELS

You will not find the city of Ur or the land of Canaan on maps today, but see if you can find Iraq and Israel on the map of the Middle East. Abraham would have travelled from Ur in Iraq to Canaan in Israel - a long way on foot!

MAKING A MAP

Abraham did not know where God was taking him, but we usually know where we are going when we set off on a journey.

Make a map of your journey from home to school.

TRAVEL DIARY

Keep a diary about the places you travel to and the distances you travel.

COLLECT CITIES

Start a collection of pictures and postcards of cities in the world.

WHIRL THE WHEEL

You will need: some thin card, two circle templates (one larger than the other), a pair of scissors, a felt tip pen and a butterfly clip.

1. Cut out two circles of thin card. One circle should be larger than the other.
2. Cut a piece out of the smaller circle as shown on the diagram.
3. Write on the smaller circle - **In faith Abraham obeyed God.**
4. Around the edge of the larger circle draw Abraham, his family, his servants and his animals.
5. Below the pictures write Ur, Haran and Shechem on three areas of the larger circle. Draw cities by the words Ur and Haran. Draw tents and a tree by the word Shechem.
   Join the two circles together with a butterfly clip.
   Move the outside circle around.

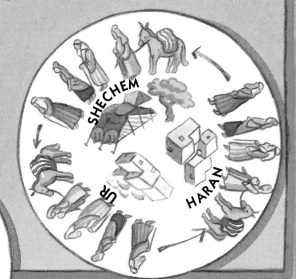

In faith Abraham obeyed God

ABRAHAM'S ADVENTURES

Read more about Abraham and how God's plan for his life worked out.
The promise of a son: **Genesis 18 v1-15 and 21 v1-8.**

WEAVING WITH WOOL

The women wove goats' hair into strips to make the tent. It must have been hard work weaving enough strips to make a whole tent.

You will need a polystyrene food tray and a ball of wool.

1. Make the slits as shown.
2. Attach a long piece of wool to the container and wind it round using the slits.
3. Take a small ball of wool, tie it onto the first strand and then weave under and over the strands. If you run out of wool, tie another piece in. (Use different colours if you wish.)
4. Weave a piece of cloth. Tie a knot at the end.
5. Use your woven cloth as a wall hanging or a coaster or a plant pot stand.

MAKE A STAR

Cut two triangles out of card and stick one on top of the other to make a star.

FIND OUT ABOUT YOUR FAMILY

How many of your relatives' names can you write down?

Fold a piece of paper as shown and cut out the shape of a person in all the layers at once. Open out the paper and discover lots of people holding hands!

Write your relatives' names on the people.

Can you find out anything about your ancestors?
Perhaps you could ask one of your older relatives about them.

SAND AND STARS

God promised Abraham that he would have as many descendants as there are stars in the sky or grains of sand along the sea-shore!

God kept his promise. All the Jewish people who have ever lived are descendants of Abraham!

Find out about the stars in the sky. You will be amazed.

Did you know that about 6,000 stars can be seen from earth without using a telescope, but there are billions of stars in our galaxy!

How many stars can you find on this page?

Answer on page 64

KNOW YOUR NAME

Can you write Abraham in Hebrew?

אַבְרָהָם

Start here

(Hebrew starts at the right!)
Abraham means 'Father of millions'.
Sarah means 'Princess'.

Do you or any of your friends have names that are found in the Bible?
See if you can find out their meaning.
A famous American president was called Abraham.
Find out what his surname was.

Answer on page 64

Siege and

Joshua looked across the River Jordan to the land of Canaan - the land which God had promised to Abraham. Joshua had dreamt of living in this Promised Land during his childhood in Egypt, where God's people had lived in slavery. But God hadn't forgotten his promise. He had sent Moses to lead the Israelites out of Egypt.

'A land flowing with milk and honey'. That is how Joshua had described Canaan when, as a young man, he had been sent there as one of Moses' spies. How he had longed then to live there, but the other spies had been frightened to invade.

Forty years passed and now Joshua was the leader of God's people and the time had come to occupy Canaan. God told Joshua, 'Get ready to cross the Jordan. I am going to give you the land. Be determined and confident. I am with you.'

JERICHO

Jericho is one of the oldest cities in the ancient world. People had settled there thousands of years before the time of Joshua! It was destroyed and rebuilt several times before Joshua captured it around 1230 BC.

In New Testament times rich people used to move to Jericho for the winter because of its milder climate. Herod the Great had his winter palace there and remains of pools and fountains from his beautiful gardens have been found. Jericho's freshwater spring makes it an oasis town in the surrounding desert and it is often known as 'the city of palms.'

DID YOU KNOW?

Did you know that the walls of Jericho were wide enough to build a house in!

WARFARE

The Israelites were constantly fighting the Canaanites to conquer the Promised Land and later to protect it from other invaders. At the time of Joshua, the main weapon used by Israelite soldiers was a single-edged sword. It was almost 300 years later before armour, bows and arrows were introduced. Their enemies, the Canaanites and the Philistines, had better weapons and chariots, which gave them an advantage in battle on open ground.

The Israelites believed that God would give them the land of Canaan and their faith gave them confidence. Their tactics included ambushes, sieges, night raids and the use of spies.

victory

So Joshua led the people across the river. The walled city of Jericho was ahead of them. The gates were kept firmly shut, for the people of Jericho were terrified of the Israelites and their God. Joshua followed God's battle plan carefully. Once a day, for six days, Joshua's men marched around the city walls in silence. The inhabitants heard no war cries or voices, just the tramping of feet and the blast of trumpets. The quivering Canaanites peered over the walls anxiously and watched the silent army.

On the seventh day the army did seven circuits, then gave a tremendous shout and the walls of Jericho collapsed! The Israelites stormed in and completely destroyed the city. The first city in the Promised Land belonged to the people of God.

Find this story in the Bible in Joshua 6 v1-20.

TRUMPETS AND HORNS

Trumpets and horns made of ram's horn were blown when Joshua's men marched around the walls of Jericho. There were several types of trumpet in Bible times. Horns were made of wood or metal. The priest's trumpet was made of gold, silver, copper or bronze. The most frequently mentioned trumpet is the shophar. It was made from a ram's horn which curled up at the end. It was used as a signal, rather than to make music. It could be used to raise an army, warn of danger or to frighten the enemy.

The shophar is still used in Jewish synagogues today.

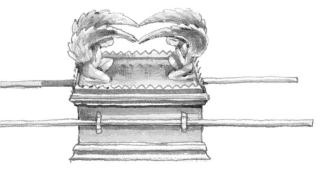

THE COVENANT BOX

Seven priests blowing trumpets headed the procession around Jericho. Behind them came four priests carrying the Covenant Box. The box was a symbol of God's presence leading his people. It was a wooden box covered with gold. On top were two cherubs and inside were the Ten Commandments, written on two stone slabs.

JERICHO STORIES

Joshua captured the city of Jericho, but this isn't the only time Jericho is mentioned in the Bible. Jesus visited Jericho several times. He healed a blind man who lived in Jericho.

Read about it in Luke 18 v35-43.
Can you find another story in Luke's gospel that took place in Jericho?
(Clue: It is about a small man who climbed a tree to see Jesus.)

Answer on page 64

FAMOUS WALLS

The strong walls of Jericho crumbled and Jericho isn't a walled city any longer. But there have been many other famous walls in the world. Here are the names of four of the most famous:

1. The Wailing Wall in Jerusalem
2. The Great Wall of China
3. Hadrian's Wall in Britain
4. The Berlin Wall in Germany

Can you match the following facts to the correct wall?

a) This wall was named after a Roman emperor, who ordered it to be built in AD122.
b) This wall is the longest wall in the world. It is 3,460 km (2,150 miles) long.
c) This wall has recently been dismantled. People died trying to get over it from one part of a city to another.
d) This wall is sacred to the Jews. It is all that remains of a temple built by King Herod 2,000 years ago.

Answers on page 64

Do you live near a famous wall or walled city that you could visit?

FLIP BOOK

Watch Jericho's walls collapse!
You will need 10 small pieces of paper and a pencil.

On the first piece of paper draw the complete walls of Jericho.
On the second page draw them collapsing a little.
Your drawing should show more crumbling on page 3.
By the time you reach page 10 the walls should have collapsed completely.
Staple the pages together. 'Flip' the book and watch the walls collapse.

MILK AND HONEY

Joshua pictured the Promised Land as a land flowing with milk and honey! To the Israelites this meant a land of abundance and plenty. It meant plenty of pasture for the sheep, cattle and goats. When there was a lot of milk, cream could be made. Honey was widely used to sweeten food. When milk and honey were mixed, a special delicacy was created.
Try this recipe to get an idea of what it would have been like.

Honey Banana Whizz

2 tablespoons of honey
150 ml natural yogurt. (Remember yogurt is made from milk)
1 large banana
2 tablespoons of lemon juice.

Mash up the banana with a fork. Beat in the lemon juice and honey.
Stir in the yogurt.
Serve. There should be enough for two.

Perhaps milk and honey are not your idea of lovely foods.

How would you have described the Promised Land to show you thought it was wonderful?
Perhaps as a land flowing with cola and hamburgers!
Think of some ideas.

SEVEN SUMS

Joshua's army walked around Jericho once a day for six days. On the seventh day they walked around Jericho seven times. Can you work out how many times Joshua walked around Jericho?

The number seven was thought to be a special, complete and perfect number in Bible times.

Here are seven Bible sums. See if you can work out the answers.

You can use a Bible and a calculator to help you!

1. The number of loaves and fish in John 6 v9 multiplied by the number of baskets of bread left over in John 6 v13.
2. The number of books in the Old Testament added to the number of books in the New Testament.
3. The number of men Jesus sent out in Luke 10 v1 subtracted from the number of fish Simon Peter caught in John 21 v11.
4. The number of the last psalm divided by the number of lepers Jesus healed in Luke 17 v17.
5. The number of times Peter denied knowing Jesus added to the number of times the cock crowed in Mark 14 v72.
   Multiply your answer by the number of helpers chosen in Acts 6 v3.
6. The number of disciples Jesus chose in Matthew 4 v18-22 multiplied by the number of sheep the shepherd had to start with in Luke 15 v4.
   Divide this by the number of coins the woman had to start with in Luke 15 v8.
7. Add up the answers to the first six sums. Add the three digits of your answer together and then add 1.

Answers on page 64

SPIRAL AROUND THE CITY

Joshua and his men walked round and round Jericho. See if you can illustrate the story. You will need a piece of paper, a piece of thread, scissors, a pencil, crayons/felt tips and something circular to draw round.

a) Draw around your circular object on your piece of paper. (A plate would do.)
b) Draw a spiral on your paper, as in the diagram.
c) Draw Jericho in the centre. Draw pin-men encircling Jericho.
d) Cut out the spiral. Attach it to a piece of thread and hang it up.

A PEBBLE COLLECTION

When the Israelites crossed the River Jordan they made a pile of twelve large stones to remind people in the future of how God had led his people into the Promised Land.

Collect twelve pebbles. Paint the faces of your family and friends on them. Thank God for your family and friends and use the pebbles to help you to remember to pray for them.

MAKE A PICTURE

Read what Joshua said in Joshua 24 v15.
AS FOR MY FAMILY AND ME, WE WILL SERVE THE LORD.
Sew this verse in cross-stitch onto a piece of material.
Here is a diagram to help you with the first letter.
If you do not like sewing, perhaps you could paint the verse or print it out on a computer.

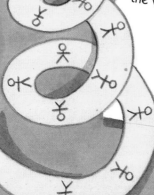

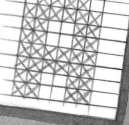

The shep

A SHEPHERD'S JOB

A shepherd looked after a mixed flock of sheep and goats and it was hard, lonely work. He had to watch over his flock day and night to protect them from wild animals, such as bears, jackals, wolves, lions, leopards and hyenas as well as from thieves and rough weather. He had to rescue sheep from dangerous places and search for any that strayed. The land was often dry and stony, but the shepherd had to find water and grass for his flock.

Sheep were usually kept for their wool, rather than for their meat. This meant that a shepherd kept each animal for a long time and got to know it. A good shepherd could recognise each of his animals and gave each one a name. They would know their master's voice and follow him.

Many years had passed since Joshua's victory at Jericho but the Israelites still had battles to fight. Their king, Saul, led his army against the fierce Philistines. His soldiers included seven brothers, all tall strong men. They had a younger brother, David, who looked after his father Jesse's sheep in the hills around Bethlehem.

In summer David slept outside and in winter he wrapped his shepherd's cloak around him and slept in the sheepfold or in a cave. David knew each of his sheep by name. They followed him along paths that led to green pastures and fresh water.

David knew he needed God's help and protection. He risked his life facing lions and bears who attacked his flock. David loved God and sometimes in the quietness of the countryside he played his harp and composed songs of

THE SHEEPFOLD

A sheepfold was built of stone. The walls were quite high and thorn branches were put along the top. The sheep were put in the sheepfold at night for protection. The shepherd slept across the entrance.

herd king

praise to God.

'The Lord is my shepherd,' sang David. 'There is nothing that I need.'

One day the prophet Samuel arrived at Jesse's home. God had told Samuel that one of Jesse's sons was to be the next king of Israel! Samuel looked at each of David's older, taller and stronger brothers. God told Samuel that none of them were to be king, for God judged not by how a person looked but by their thoughts. God chose David, the youngest and the smallest in the family to be the next king. No one in the family forgot that day!

You will find David's shepherd song in the Bible in Psalm 23 v1-6. The story of how David was chosen to be the next king is in 1 Samuel 16 v1-13.

A SHEPHERD'S TOOLS

A shepherd wore a camel-hair cloak to protect himself from the weather and carried a small bag with food such as cheese, bread, raisins and olives.

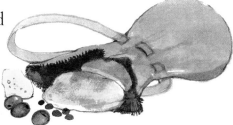

♦ Shepherds had certain tools: A rod or club about one metre long to drive away wild animals.
♦ A shepherd's staff, two metres long and with a curved end. It was used to guide the sheep and pull them out of dangerous places.
♦ A horn filled with olive oil. When an animal was hurt the oil was put on its wounds.
♦ A sling made of leather or plaited hair to hurl stones at wild animals which threatened the sheep.

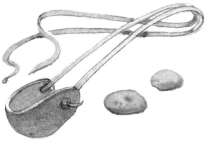

♦ A shepherd might use a dog to help him.

DID YOU KNOW?
A lamb is the only animal mentioned as a pet in the Old Testament.
Read 2 Samuel 12 v3.

THE GOOD NEWS IS …
God doesn't look at how tall, good-looking or clever we are. What counts with God is our trust in him.

KNIT A SHEEP

You will need some thin card, an envelope, some wool, knitting needles, glue, green and black pens.

1. Cast on 10 stitches and knit about 10 rows. Cast off.
2. Stick your woolly rectangle on to your greetings card.
3. Draw a head, ears and four legs around the knitting to make a sheep.
4. Use your green pen to draw grass and to write
   THE LORD IS MY SHEPHERD.

If you cannot knit, draw a sheep shape on your card and stick pieces of wool or cotton wool on to the body of the sheep instead.

5. Give the card to a friend.

GROW A SHEEP

You will need some cress seeds, a plate and a piece of kitchen roll or blotting paper.

1. Cut the shape of a sheep in kitchen roll or blotting paper.
   You may like to colour the head in black.
2. Put the picture on to the plate. Dampen the body of the sheep.
3. Sprinkle the cress seeds carefully on to the body of the sheep.
4. Wait for your sheep to grow cress for wool! (Remember to keep the paper damp.)
5. "Shear" your sheep. Wash the "wool" and eat it!

FINGERPRINT FLOCK

No one has the same fingerprints as you! Everyone is unique!
Use an ink pad and put some of your fingerprints on to a piece of paper. Use your pen to make fingerprint sheep.
Write the following on the paper, to remind yourself you are a one off!

GOD'S LOVE AND GOODNESS WILL BE WITH ME ALL THE DAYS OF MY LIFE BECAUSE THERE IS NO ONE ELSE LIKE ME! PSALM 23 v6.

SHEEP VISITS

Can you visit a farm or go and watch a sheep-dog demonstration?

A SHEPHERD'S STAFF

Who carries a shepherd's staff today, but does not look after sheep?

Answer on page 64

SHEEP FACTS

Is it true or false?

1. Australia has the most sheep in the world (140 million!).
2. Female sheep are called ewes and male sheep are called rams.
3. Merino sheep have the finest wool.
4. Meat from an adult sheep is called mutton.
5. Wool comes from goats, sheep, alpacas, vicunas and rabbits.
6. An expert shearer with a pair of electric clippers can shear a sheep in 40 seconds!
7. There are 20 sheep for every human being in New Zealand!
8. The wealth of a man in biblical times was measured by the size of his flock.

Answers on page 64
Can you find out any more sheep facts?

GOD'S WORLD

David spent a lot of his time in the beautiful countryside that God had created.
Do you ever spend time out in the country?

Appreciate God's creation when you go out walking and don't spoil it.

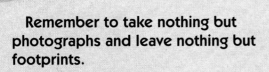

Remember to take nothing but photographs and leave nothing but footprints.

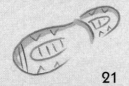

Make a list of ways people damage the environment and think of one or two practical ways to care for God's world.

SHEEP MOBILE

You will need a wire coat hanger, thread and some thin card.

1. Cut out six sheep from the card. Draw in their faces.
2. Write a verse from Psalm 23 on each sheep.
3. Put a thread through the back of each sheep and tie it to the wire coat hanger.

A SHEPHERD'S SLING

David was an accurate shot with his sling.
He also had faith in God.
Read how this combination brought him victory in
1 Samuel 17 v1-58.

Making

MUSICAL INSTRUMENTS

Many musical instruments are mentioned in the Bible, for example in Psalm 150. There were three groups of musical instruments in Israel - string, wind and percussion.

STRINGS

David often played a small eight or ten stringed lyre with a frame made of cypress wood. It was played with the fingers or a plectrum.

Other stringed instruments were harps, zithers, psalteries and lutes.

WIND

A flute was rather like a recorder, but it did not produce a very musical sound.

The pipe was the most popular wind instrument. It could make both sad and joyful sounds. Trumpets and horns were also wind instruments.

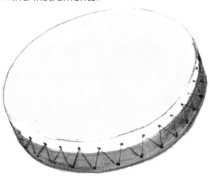

'Long live King David!' shouted the Israelites, as they celebrated the start of his reign. The prophet Samuel had anointed David king when he was only a shepherd boy. Now it was time for him to take up his throne.

David needed a capital city where he could set up his royal court. He chose Jerusalem, a fortress high on a hill, which belonged to his enemies, the Jebusites.

'You'll never get in here!' the Jebusites taunted David's men. 'Even the blind could keep you out!' But David's men crawled up through the water tunnel and took the Jebusites by surprise. Jerusalem became 'David's City'.

David wanted it to be 'God's City' and so he had the Covenant Box, containing the laws of Moses, brought to the new capital in a triumphant procession. Choirs sang, harps, lyres, drums and cymbals were played, while David and the

PERCUSSION

There were two kinds of cymbals - loud cymbals and high sounding cymbals. Both were used in worship.

A timbrel was like a small drum or tambourine made from two skins stretched over a wooden hoop. It was played by women.

The sistrum, rattle or castanet had a wooden frame with wires across it. The wires had metal discs on them which rattled when shaken.

music

THE GOOD NEWS IS ...
David had confidence in God's guidance. We too can talk to God and rely on him to show us the right things to do in our lives.

Israelites danced in the streets!

'Sing praise to the Lord and proclaim his greatness! Tell of the wonderful things he has done!' sang David and the Israelites.

David reigned in Israel for more than thirty years. He had learnt to rely on God when he was a shepherd and he continued to rely on him when he became king. He talked to God before he fought battles and had confidence in the Lord's protection and guidance. He ruled fairly, dealing with everyone equally.

David wrote many of the psalms in our Bible. In them he writes honestly about his mistakes and fears as well as his hopes and joys.

The story of how David brought the Covenant Box to Jerusalem is in 2 Samuel 6 v1-5.

MUSIC MAKERS

Musicians were important people in ancient Israel. David organised a choir and an orchestra of harps, horns, cymbals and trumpets to worship God. They used the psalms in worship.

Music was also a part of everyday life. Joyful songs were sung at weddings, feasts and after a victory in battle. There were sad mournful songs for funerals. People sang as they worked. The Bible mentions songs sung by people planting grapes and digging wells!

DID YOU KNOW?

When the Israelites worshipped God, they sang, played many different musical instruments and even shouted! One of the Hebrew words for praise means 'to make a noise'.

DANCING

The Israelites loved dancing! People danced to thank God for a good harvest or a victory in battle and they danced for fun at parties and celebrations. Men and women danced separately.

WRITE A SONG

David wrote many songs or psalms which expressed to God exactly how he felt.
Some were happy, joyful songs and some were sad and quiet.
See if you can write the words and music for a song.
Can you record your song on a tape recorder?

MAKE MUSICAL INSTRUMENTS

On the previous page are drawings of several different types of musical instrument, used in Israel. Many everyday things can be used to make music.
Here are some ideas. Perhaps you can think of some of your own?

a) A COMB MOUTH-ORGAN

You will need a comb and some greaseproof paper or tissue paper.
Put the paper over the comb and blow through the paper. What kind of sounds can you make? Try creating a tune and using different types of comb.

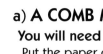

b) A TISSUE BOX HARP

You will need an empty tissue box, two pieces of wood or polystyrene and some elastic bands of different thicknesses (but the same length).
Put the wood or polystyrene on top of the box. Stretch the elastic bands round the box and space them out. Pluck your harp!

c) A DRIED PEA RATTLE

You will need some dried peas or lentils and a plastic container with a lid. A small plastic fizzy drinks bottle would do.
Put the peas inside the container. Shake it! You could cover your rattle with decorated paper.

d) A BOTTLE TOP AND BUTTON TAMBOURINE

You will need to collect some bottle tops and flatten them. Ask an adult to make a hole in them.
You will also need a piece of wire and some buttons.
Thread the bottle tops and buttons on to the wire and join into a circle. Shake the 'tambourine.'

e) A GREASEPROOF PAPER DRUM

You will need some greaseproof paper, a round or square tin and some sellotape.
Stretch some greaseproof paper over the tin and fasten it with sellotape. You have a drum. Tap rhythms on it with your fingers.

f) BOTTLE FLUTES

You will need some empty glass bottles and some water.
Put different amounts of water in each bottle. Blow across the top of each bottle. Air vibrates in each bottle to make a sound.
Which bottles make high sounds and which make low sounds?
Can you 'blow' or tap a tune?

JUST A NOTE

Send a musical note to a friend!
Get a piece of writing paper and decorate the edges of it with musical notes.
Write 'A note for you . . .' at the top of the paper.
Write a letter or note to a friend.

BIBLE SONGS

David was not the only one who composed songs that are recorded in the Bible. Look up these songs.
Moses - Exodus 15 v1-18
Miriam - Exodus 15 v20-21
Mary - Luke 1 v46-55
The Angels - Luke 2 v14

FACES

David knew he could talk to God however he was feeling.
Cut out some circles of paper. Use these as faces and draw expressions on them.
How many can you do? Here are some ideas to start you off.
No matter how you are feeling, you can talk to God and he will listen.
Talk to God now and tell him how you feel.
You can use the words of David's psalms to express your feelings to God.
When you want to say sorry, use Psalm 51 v1-2.
When you want to say thank you to God, use Psalm 34 v1-3.
When you want to praise God, use Psalm 150 v1-2.

BE A CHEERLEADER

In America cheerleaders dance, chant and cheer on their favourite football teams while waving streamers. David danced, chanted and cheered for God!
You will need two cardboard tubes (the inside of a toilet roll or kitchen roll) some felt pens, sellotape and streamers.
Decorate the tubes.
Stick lengths of streamers to one end of each tube.
Make up a march or a dance routine. Wave your streamers and choose some lines of the song David sang in the procession with the Covenant Box. You will find David's song in the Bible in 1 Chronicles 16 v8-36. Or sing Psalm 150 or your favourite Christian song.

HALF A GUITAR

Many instruments are symmetrical. (Symmetrical means both sides are exactly alike.)
To make a symmetrical guitar you will need some scissors, paints and a piece of paper.
Fold the paper in half and draw half the guitar close to the folded edge of the paper.
Cut around the outline. Open the paper and see a whole, symmetrical guitar. Use your paints to paint the guitar.
Are any other instruments symmetrical?

CAPITAL CITIES

David chose Jerusalem as his capital city. It is still the capital city of Israel. What can you find out about Jerusalem?

Can you match the capital city with its country?

1. London
2. Washington DC
3. Paris
4. Cairo
5. Rome

a) Italy
b) Egypt
c) England
d) France
e) USA

Answers on page 64.

SING-A-LONG

David probably sang while he was a shepherd because music was popular and people sang when they were working.
Read the somg that was sung when a well was being dug - it is in the Bible in Numbers 21 v17-18.
Perhaps you whistle as you walk along, or hum while you are in the car.
Make up a song for washing the car, having a bath, doing the washing up, walking the dog, riding a bicycle, posting a letter or some other situation.

A Temple

'What would you like me to give you?' God asked Solomon, when he became king of Israel.

'Please give me the wisdom I need to rule your people,' answered Solomon.

'I am pleased that you have asked for wisdom, rather than wealth, long life or power,' replied God. 'I will give you more wisdom and understanding than anyone has ever had! I will also give you riches!'

Solomon's knowledge was so great it couldn't be measured. He wrote three thousand proverbs and more than a thousand songs!

Solomon also became rich. He had forty thousand stalls for his chariot horses and a fleet of ocean-going ships. His throne was made of ivory and gold and carved with lions. Even his drinking cups were made of gold! Solomon began work on a Temple for God. More than one hundred and ninety thousand men were employed to build the Temple.

The stone for the Temple was prepared at the quarry. There was to be no noise made by hammers or other tools at the Temple site. Inside, the walls were covered with cedar panels, overlaid with gold. Each panel was decorated with carvings of flowers, palm trees and cherubim. The Covenant Box was placed in the Most Holy Place at the rear of the Temple.

When the Temple was completed, Solomon summoned all the leaders of Israel to a great ceremony of dedication to God.

Find the story of how Solomon built the Temple in 1 Kings chapters 5-8.

THE PRIESTS

The Israelites were divided into twelve tribes. The tribe of Levi performed religious duties in the Temple as doorkeepers or sang in the choir or played in the orchestra.

Those Levites who were descended from Aaron could become priests at the age of thirty. They wore special clothes and prayed and offered sacrifices on behalf of the people. The priests also taught God's laws.

The High Priest was able to go into the Most Holy Place once a year on the Day of Atonement. The job of High Priest was passed from father to son.

TEMPLE FURNITURE

The tall stone altar was where sacrifices were made.

An enormous bronze basin was used by the priests for washing before entering the Temple. Carved doors in the entrance hall opened into the biggest room.

In the Holy Place there were golden candlesticks, the incense altar and a table on which sat twelve loaves.

The Covenant Box was found in the Most Holy Place.

Storerooms were used for the priests' clothes, the treasury and offerings.

for God

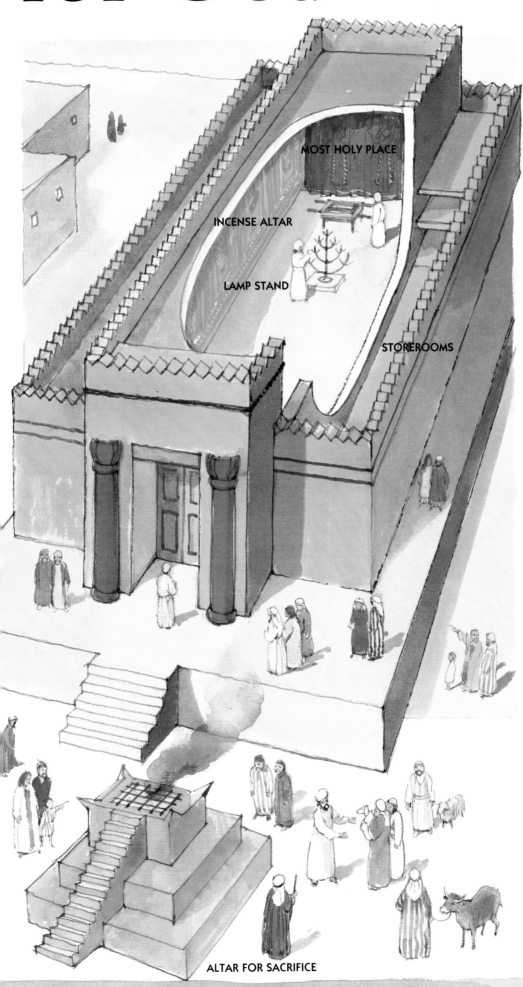

MOST HOLY PLACE

INCENSE ALTAR

LAMP STAND

STOREROOMS

ALTAR FOR SACRIFICE

SOLOMON'S TEMPLE

Solomon built the Temple in Jerusalem as a house for God, not a meeting place for God's people. Only the priests were allowed inside, but all the Israelites were expected to visit the Temple courtyard for sacrifices, great feasts and celebrations.

It was not a huge building. It was nine metres wide, twenty-seven metres long and about fourteen metres high. It was quite dark inside, as there were only small, high windows and candles. The Most Holy Place was completely dark.

Solomon's Temple was destroyed by King Nebuchadnezzar of Babylon in 586 BC. God's people rebuilt it in 515 BC, but this second Temple was not as magnificent as Solomon's. It was destroyed in 63 BC by the Roman general, Pompey.

SACRIFICES AND OFFERINGS

Sacrifices of animals were offered to God in thanksgiving or praise or when a person had sinned. Only the best animals could be presented to God. Offerings of flour, oil or grain were made by the poor. Prayer was also very important in Temple worship.

DID YOU KNOW?

Solomon began to build the Temple in 957 BC. It took seven years to complete.

FAMOUS BUILDINGS

King Solomon's Temple must have been very beautiful inside. Where do you find these famous and fine buildings? Match the building with its city.

1. Notre Dame
2. The Empire State Building
3. The White House
4. The Kremlin
5. Buckingham Palace

a. London
b. Paris
c. New York
d. Washington DC
e. Moscow

Which of these famous buildings is a place of worship?

Answers on page 64

PRAISE HIM PRAYER

Solomon praised God with a prayer when the Temple was finished. Write a prayer of praise to God for all the good things he has done for you. Start each line with the words -
I praise you Lord God for . . .

TEMPLE STORIES

Jesus visited Herod's Temple in Jerusalem when he was on earth.
Read some of the stories of Jesus' visits.
Luke 2 v 41-49. Jesus as a boy.
Mark 11 v 15-17. Jesus drives out the merchants.
Luke 21 v 1-4. The widow's offering.

PEACE AND QUIET

Solomon's Temple was put up without the sound of a hammer, axe or any other tool. This was because God is holy and keeping quiet was a sign of respect for God. Sometimes we can concentrate better if it is quiet.

Make a DO NOT DISTURB sign for your bedroom door. Hang it on the door handle when you want a quiet time to talk to God in.

RULERS AND LEADERS

Match the name to the description.
1. Julius Caesar
2. George Washington
3. Nicholas II
4. Henry VIII

a. an English king who had six wives
b. a Roman emperor
c. the first president of America
d. Russia's last czar who was murdered in 1918

History books judge these rulers and leaders on the things they achieved, but the Bible sees a leader's relationship with God as the most important thing.

Answers on page 64

BUILDING OR BODIES?

Solomon called his Temple God's house, even though he knew it wasn't big enough for God to live in. The followers of Jesus did not have special buildings to meet in but met in each other's houses.
Although we have buildings that are called churches, people who love God are called the church too. So the word church means both a building and people!
Draw a church shape and fill it with people's faces.

SOLOMON'S SPLENDOUR

Solomon was very rich and owned many splendid treasures but Jesus said that something God created is even more wonderful.
Find out what in Matthew 6 v 28-29.
Place some flower petals inside a newspaper. Carefully pile some heavy books on top of the paper. Leave it for a week.
Use the pressed flowers to make a bookmark, or a card for a friend.

PHOENICIAN SHIPS

You will need some stiff card, material, a stick, some string, straws, glue and paint.
The Phoenicians were the best sailors in the ancient world. Solomon asked for their help to build his fleet of ships.
The ships had a horse's head at the prow and a fish's tail at the stern. They had oars and one large sail. These ships sailed long distances. Some even reached Britain!
See if you can make a Phoenician galley ship.

LOGS

Cedar logs for the wood panels in Solomon's Temple came from Lebanon. Men chopped down trees and dragged the logs to the sea. The logs were then float-ed to the port of Joppa!
Today the country of Canada exports a lot of timber. Their logs are also floated down rivers. Men balance on the logs and guide them with long poles.

Can you find out:
1. what these men are called?
2. what some of Canada's logs are used for?
3. how you can tell how old a tree is?
Answers on page 64

STAINED GLASS

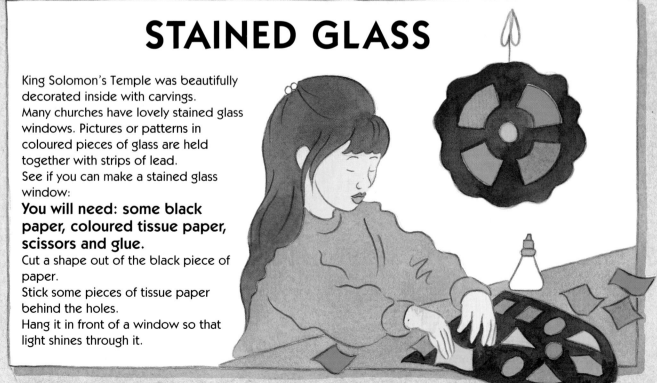

King Solomon's Temple was beautifully decorated inside with carvings.
Many churches have lovely stained glass windows. Pictures or patterns in coloured pieces of glass are held together with strips of lead.
See if you can make a stained glass window:
You will need: some black paper, coloured tissue paper, scissors and glue.
Cut a shape out of the black piece of paper.
Stick some pieces of tissue paper behind the holes.
Hang it in front of a window so that light shines through it.

The king

King Ahab of Israel was wicked and disobeyed God's laws. His wife, Jezebel, encouraged him to do every sort of evil and to worship other gods.

One of his subjects, called Naboth, owned a vineyard close to Ahab's palace.

'I want your vineyard to use as a vegetable garden,' said King Ahab to Naboth. 'I will give you another vineyard or pay you whatever it is worth.'

But Naboth replied, 'This vineyard has been in my family for generations. It would be wrong for me to sell it. You cannot have it.'

Ahab was furious. He went back to his palace, lay on his bed with his face to the wall and refused to eat.

'What's the matter, Ahab?' asked Jezebel. 'Why won't you eat?'

'I want Naboth's vineyard and he won't give it to me!' said Ahab sulkily.

'You are the king!' exclaimed Jezebel angrily. 'You shall have the land.'

Jezebel thought and schemed and came up with a nasty plan. She wrote a letter to the important men of Jezreel and signed it in Ahab's name. The letter ordered them to accuse Naboth of speaking against God and Ahab. Naboth was put on trial, found guilty and stoned to death.

Jezebel went and told Ahab the news. 'Naboth is dead! The vineyard is yours!' she said gleefully.

So Ahab hurried eagerly to see his new vineyard. At the entrance to the land stood Elijah, God's messenger.

'I have a message from God,' said Elijah sternly. 'You and Jezebel have murdered Naboth and seized his property. God will punish you for your wickedness.'

WINE MAKING

There was only a limited choice of drinks in Bible times. There was milk from the family goat, vinegar mixed with water, fruit juice, water or wine.

Grape juice was made from freshly squeezed grapes during harvest time. But wine was the favourite drink, so most of the harvested grapes were taken to the wine press. They were trampled by barefooted workers who sang as they worked. The juice was squeezed out of the grapes and flowed into another small container. This juice had to ferment for six weeks. All the skins and stalks sank to the bottom and formed a sludge known as 'lees'. When the wine was ready, it was put in large pottery jars or goatskins.

DID YOU KNOW?

In Bible times there was a law which said, "When you walk along a path in someone else's vineyard, you may eat all the grapes you want, but you must not carry any away in a container." Read this law in Deuteronomy 23 v24.

who sulked

Ahab knew what Elijah said was true and he felt sorry. He realised he had broken God's holy laws so he dressed in sackcloth and ate no food to show his sorrow. God noticed and did not punish him, but Ahab continued to sin against God.

AHAB AND JEZEBEL

After King Solomon died the land of Israel was split in two. There was a northern kingdom called Israel and a southern kingdom called Judah. Each part had its own king. The kings who ruled the northern kingdom were all wicked, but Ahab was one of the worst. Jezebel got the Israelites to worship a god called Baal instead of the one true God. Elijah, God's messenger, constantly warned Ahab and Jezebel about their wrongdoing and they hated him for it. Elijah challenged the prophets of Baal to a contest to prove who was the real God. This exciting story can be found in 1 KIngs 18.

OLD TESTAMENT LAWS

Many of God's laws were written down in the Old Testament books of Leviticus and Deuteronomy.

King Ahab and Queen Jezebel broke several of these laws when they were dealing with Naboth. Firstly, the land was God's gift to his people and they were not to sell it. Ahab knew the law but he still wanted to buy Naboth's land. Secondly, two witnesses were necessary to prove a person guilty. But the judge was to check if the story was true. If not, the accuser was to be punished instead. Jezebel's witnesses were false and she lied about Naboth, but there was no investigation and Naboth died unjustly.

THE GOOD NEWS IS ... God treats everybody the same way. People who are rich and powerful like King Ahab are the same in God's eyes as ordinary people like Naboth. God loves us all equally and he wants everyone to keep his standards of behaviour.

VINEYARD STORY

Jesus told a story about workers in a vineyard.
Read about it in Matthew 20 v1-16

MATCH THE PAIRS

Match the words and their meanings.

1. Vine
2. Vineyard
3. Viticulture
4. A vine dresser

a. A vine plantation
b. Vine growing
c. Someone whose job it is to grow vines
d. A grape bearing plant

Answers on page 64

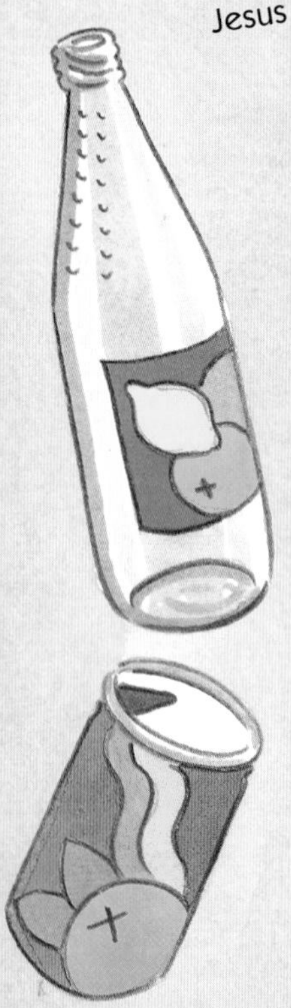

BOTTLES AND CANS

Unlike people in Bible times we have a wide choice of drinks to choose from.
See how many you can name. Most of our drinks are packaged in glass or plastic bottles or aluminium cans.

Glass, aluminium and plastic can be recycled and used again. Start saving cans and bottles. Then take them to your local recycling centre.

CREATE A COASTER

Sometimes drinks leave marks on furniture, so coasters are a good idea.
You will need some card, scissors, colouring pens and sticky-backed plastic.
1. Cut out a circle of card.
2. Draw a bunch of grapes or other fruit on the card and colour it in.
3. Cover the card in clear sticky backed plastic.

LETTERS

Jezebel wrote a letter which was nasty and on which she faked Ahab's signature. The letter caused a lot of harm.
Letters can create a lot of happiness though. Why not write a letter to one of your grandparents or a friend you haven't seen for a while?
Find out about the history of letters, stamps and post boxes.
Start a stamp collection.

RAISE A RAISIN

Many grapes in Israel were dried in the sun to make raisins. Raisins are just dried grapes!

Raisins were easy to take as food on journeys.

Read what Abigail gave King David in 1 Samuel 25 v18.

Put some fizzy drink in a glass. Drop some raisins in and watch what happens.

The bubbles attach themselves to the raisins and the gas in them is so light that it carries the raisins to the top of the glass! The bubbles burst at the top, so the raisins sink.

MAKE SOME MUESLI

Muesli is a very healthy breakfast cereal which you can make. You will need:
125g rolled oats
125g chopped nuts
125g seedless raisins
50g soft brown sugar

Mix all the ingredients. Serve with milk.

SEEDS, PIPS, STONES

Make a fruit salad. While you are doing it, collect the pips inside grapes and other fruit such as melon, oranges, apples and kiwi fruit.

Dry some of the pips and glue them onto paper to make pictures.
You could make a necklace out of dried melon seeds.

Find out about seeds, pips and stones and how they disperse.
Make a collection of as many different seeds as you can.

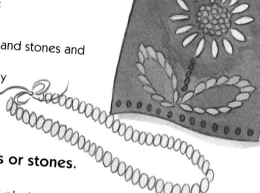

Grow some seeds, pips or stones.
Here are some suggestions -
Grapes - Dry the seeds and plant several in a pot. Water them.
Oranges - Plant a pip in a pot. Keep the pot in a warm, dark place. When you see the shoots, move the pot to a sunny window sill. Water it.
Avocado - Put the stone in water for a day to soften it. Push two cocktail sticks into it so that you can balance it on a jar with the wide end of the stone just covered in water. Put the jar on the window sill and don't let the water level go down. When a shoot starts to grow, remove the sticks and plant the stone in a pot.
Peanut - Shell the nuts and plant them in a pot on a warm windowsill. Water them.

Grapes, oranges and avocados are all grown in Israel today.
You will be able to grow nice leafy plants but no fruit.
You may manage to grow your own peanuts though!

Another plant that is fun to grow is the sunflower.
Follow the instructions on the seed packet carefully and you may manage to grow a plant that is much taller than you!

A VEGETABLE PATCH

Ahab wanted Naboth's land for a vegetable or herb garden.
If your family have a garden, ask if you could have a small part of it to grow vegetables or herbs in.
If you don't have a garden, perhaps you can grow something in a tub or a window box.

If your parents say no, don't behave like Ahab or Jezebel!

If your parents say yes, buy some seeds and read the instructions on the packet carefully before you plant them.

THE GOOD NEWS IS ...
Gabriel told Mary and
Zechariah that nothing is
impossible for God! That is
still true today!

Two babies

The Jews had waited for many years for the saviour God had promised to send. Some gave up hope, others believed that God would keep his promise. Among these were Zechariah, a priest, and his wife, Elizabeth.

One day when Zechariah was working in the Temple, the angel Gabriel appeared beside the altar. Zechariah was frightened, but Gabriel said, 'Do not be afraid - God is going to give you and Elizabeth a son. You must name him John and he will prepare the way for the saviour.'

'It's impossible! Elizabeth and I are too old to have a baby,' Zechariah said in disbelief.

'God sent me to deliver this happy news to you!' Gabriel replied. 'But because you have not believed it, you will be unable to speak until the baby is born.'

It all happened just as Gabriel had said.

CHILDREN'S GAMES

Homes had small windows and were dark inside, so children played outside in the market-place or on the hillside. They played imaginary games of weddings and funerals. Games such as hide-and-seek, tug-of-war and blind man's buff were also known. Telling riddles was a popular pastime and people of all ages enjoyed trying to solve them.

Israelite children had no dolls, but they did have balls, rattles, hoops, whistles and spinning tops. Lines for hopscotch have been found in Pilate's fortress in Jerusalem. Dice have also been found by archaeologists. Board games are never referred to in the Bible, but games similar to chess or draughts were known at the time.

BABIES

In Israel children were regarded as a gift from God and childlessness was seen as a disgrace.

Pregnant women in the ancient world could only get help from other women in the family or village. There were no hospitals or clinics, so births took place at home. After the birth the baby would be washed, rubbed down with salt and then wrapped in strips of cloth. There were no special baby clothes. The baby would be laid in a simple cradle hung from a beam or between two forked sticks. Babies were breast-fed for many months and sometimes for as long as two or three years.

and an angel

Some months later, God sent Gabriel to deliver a message to a girl called Mary who was engaged to a carpenter called Joseph.

'Peace be with you!' said Gabriel. Mary was startled.

'Don't be afraid, Mary. You will become pregnant and give birth to a son and you will name him Jesus. He will be the Son of the Most High God!'

'I am God's servant,' said Mary. 'I will do whatever God wants me to do.'

Soon after, the Emperor Augustus ordered everyone to return to the town of his ancestors for a census. Mary and Joseph travelled to Bethlehem because Joseph was a descendant of King David. While they were there, Mary gave birth to Jesus. She wrapped him in strips of cloth and laid him in a manger, because the inn was full.

Find the stories of the births of John and Jesus in Luke 1-2.

HOME EDUCATION

The first lesson a boy would learn would be the Shema. This is found in Deuteronomy 6 v4-9. Fathers taught their sons God's laws and stories of how God had led his people in the past. Boys looked after the family's flocks and learnt their father's trade.

A mother taught her daughters how to cook meals, grind corn, spin, weave and take care of children. Some girls would also look after the family's sheep and help with the harvests. Girls were usually married by the age of sixteen and so were taught how to be good wives and mothers.

SCHOOLS

Synagogue schools for boys aged six onwards became compulsory around AD 63-65. The teachers at these schools were highly respected married men known as rabbis. A rabbi would have a class of around twenty-five pupils. If a class reached forty in size, an assistant teacher would be appointed. Boys sat on the ground at the feet of their rabbi and learnt to read, write and quote the Scriptures. Hours were long and there were few school holidays.

DID YOU KNOW?

Birthdays were not celebrated in Israel!

A BEDTIME STORY

Children in Bible times were told stories by their parents about the things God had done for his people.

Do you know a small child you can go and read a bedtime story to?

BIBLE BABY STORIES

Read stories of other Bible babies like Moses who was put in a floating basket. His story is in Exodus chapter 2 verses 1-10. The story of Samuel, who was given to God, is in 1 Samuel chapter 1.

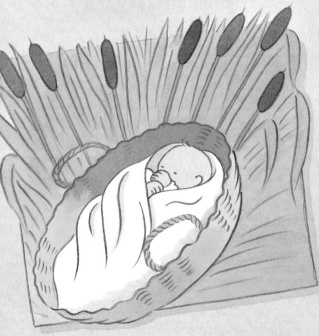

JOHN THE BAPTIST

When Zechariah and Elizabeth's baby grew up, he became known as John the Baptist. Read about his life and death - Matthew 3 v1-17, Mark 6 v14-29.

See if you can find the answers to these questions.
1. Where did John baptize?
2. What food did he eat?
3. Why did people come to be baptized?
4. What happened when John baptized Jesus?
5. How did John die?

Answers on page 64

A ROMAN CENSUS

Mary and Joseph travelled to Bethlehem because the Roman Emperor had ordered a census of all the Roman lands to be taken. A census is when the population is counted.

1. The Roman emperor who ordered the census was called Augustus. Which of our months do you think is named after him?
2. Another Roman emperor has given his name to one of our months. Who is it?

Answers on page 64

WRAPPING PAPER

Make your own Christmas wrapping paper.
You will need some brown paper (the sort you wrap parcels with) or some coloured paper, half a raw potato and some bright paint.

1. Ask an adult to cut a star out of the potato.
2. Put the potato into the paint and print some stars on the paper.
3. Let it dry and then wrap up someone's Christmas present.

STAR GIFT TAGS

Make your own gift tags for Christmas.
You will need some ribbon, scissors and thin yellow card.

1. Cut the star shape out of the card.
2. Make a hole and fasten the ribbon through the hole.
3. Write a message onto the tag and fasten it to a gift.

BABY TALK

Ask your parents if they have photographs of you or them as babies.

Find out what the first word you ever spoke was and some of the things you did when you were a baby or toddler! Make a record book entitled **The Story of my Life.**

SHALOM

The angel Gabriel greeted Zechariah and Mary with the words, "Peace be with you". In Hebrew the word 'shalom' means 'peace be with you'. It is still used as a greeting between people.

This is how you write 'shalom' in Hebrew.

שלום

Write this or **PEACE BE WITH YOU** on the shape of a dove. The dove is a symbol of peace.

Display it at the entrance to your home. It will greet all your visitors.

Miracle

Jesus was a guest at a wedding in the village of Cana in Galilee. His mother, Mary, and his disciples were also invited to the celebrations.

During the party the wine supply ran out. 'What shall we do?' said one of the servants anxiously. 'Our master will be disgraced.'

Mary overheard the servants talking, and went to tell Jesus about the problem. Then she returned to the worried servants and said, 'Do whatever Jesus tells you to do.'

There were six stone water jars standing nearby. Each of them could hold about one hundred litres.

'Fill these jars to the brim with water,' Jesus told the servants.

Although the servants did not know what Jesus was going to do, they trusted him and did exactly as he told them. They worked hard and carried pitchers of water from the well. Some time later their bodies ached, but the jars were full up.

THE BETROTHAL

It was unusual for people not to marry at the time of Jesus. The legal ages for marriage were thirteen for a boy and twelve for a girl. The parents arranged the wedding and an exchange of money was involved.

The groom's father paid the agreed 'bride price' to the girl's family. The bride's family gave her a dowry (a wedding gift). The couple were then formally betrothed in front of two witnesses. Sometimes the bridegroom gave his bride a headband of coins.

The betrothal was as binding as marriage and was very difficult to break. The betrothed couple could even be called 'husband' and 'wife'.

The period of betrothal lasted for some months or years and the wedding took place when the bridegroom had the new home ready.

DID YOU KNOW?

Wedding celebrations in the time of Jesus often lasted for at least seven days! No wonder they ran out of wine at this wedding!

THE WEDDING

The ceremony took place in the bridegroom's house. The male and female guests sat separately during the eating and drinking. The celebrations would also involve music, singing and dancing.

at Cana

'Take a cup of the water to the man in charge of the feast,' Jesus told one of the servants. The servant rather nervously did as he was told. When the man drank from the cup it was no longer water. It had turned into wine!

'This is delicious!' the man declared. 'Most people serve the best wine first, but you have kept the best wine until last!' he said to the bridegroom.

The servants, who knew where the wine had come from, smiled.

They were astonished by what Jesus had done, and were glad that they had trusted him.

This was the first of many miracles done by Jesus.

The story of how Jesus turned water into wine is in John 2 v1-11.

THE BRIDE

The bridesmaids helped the bride to get ready on her wedding day. The bride wore a richly embroidered dress and a veil which covered her face. Her face, nails, feet and hands were polished until they shone. Her hair was plaited and lengths of silk were placed in each plait. Coins were fastened to the pieces of silk. There could be hundreds of coins in her hair! She also wore jewellery which the bridegroom had given her. Sometimes he gave her a headband of coins.

THE BRIDEGROOM

The bridegroom and his friends went to the bride's house to collect the bride. Wreaths of flowers were placed on the heads of both the bride and bridegroom. The colourful procession took place in the evening. People lined the route wearing their best clothes and holding torches. There was often music and dancing along the way.

FAMILY WEDDINGS

Ask if you can see your parents' wedding photos.
Ask them about their wedding.
Ask if they have any photos
of the weddings of your
grandparents or
great grandparents.

CUPS AND STRAWS

Decorate paper cups and straws for a celebration.

PARTY HATS

Jesus enjoyed celebrating at a wedding. It was a happy occasion!

It is fun to wear party hats at a celebration or party.
These party hats are simple to make.

You will need some shiny or coloured thin card, some thin elastic, scissors, glue and something to decorate the hat with.

1. Cut out a 30cm diameter circle. Cut a slice out of the hat as in the diagram.
2. Overlap the edges and stick them down. You should have a cone shaped hat.
3. Make small holes in each side of the hat and tie a piece of elastic on to the hat.
4. Decorate the hat with sticky stars, glitter or pictures from magazines.

SPECIAL PARTY ICE CUBES

At the wedding Jesus went to, the guests drank wine. At a party or celebration there are often special things to drink.

Make some special ice cubes for party drinks .

You will need an ice-cube tray, water and some slices of strawberry.

Put a slice of strawberry in each section of the tray. Fill up with water and freeze. Add a special ice cube to your party drink!

(You could experiment with slices of other fruits, cut shapes out of lemon or orange peel or freeze coloured juice for your ice cubes.)

READ ABOUT IT

Read about a wedding in the Old Testament where the bridegroom was tricked into marrying the wrong girl! Find the story in Genesis 29 v18-30

A PRESENT OF PEPPERMINTS

People often take presents to a celebration. Make some peppermint creams to give to someone as a present.

You will need: 1lb icing sugar, the white of one egg, half a lemon and some peppermint essence, 2 bowls, a knife or cutters, teaspoon, lemon squeezer, a wooden spoon and a sieve.

1. Sift the icing sugar through the sieve into a bowl.
2. Put the egg white into a bowl with the icing sugar. Mix them with the wooden spoon.
3. Knead the mixture with clean hands until the egg white and icing sugar are blended.
4. If the mixture is crumbly and stiff add drops of lemon juice until it is pliable and bendy.
5. Add half a teaspoon of peppermint essence and mix with the wooden spoon.
6. Press the mixture out flat with your fingers on a cold surface.
   Cut into shapes and leave to set in a cold, airy place.
7. Put your peppermints into a pretty box and give them away as a gift.

MAKE A GARLAND

The bridegroom at a wedding in the time of Jesus wore a garland.

Make a garland for the guest of honour at your party (This might be the birthday boy or girl) or make one for each guest at a summer party.

You will need a necklace length of string for each garland. (This must fit over a person's head.) Some scissors and coloured tissue or crepe paper.

1. Cut the tissue paper into flower shapes and thread them onto the string until it is full.
2. Tie the ends of the string.

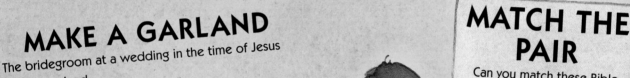

MATCH THE PAIR

Can you match these Bible husband and wife pairs?

MEN
- a) Adam
- b) Samson
- c) Abraham
- d) Jacob
- e) Isaac

WOMEN
- f) Sarah
- g) Eve
- h) Rachel
- i) Delilah
- j) Rebecca

Answers on page 64.

CELEBRATIONS

Make a list of the special times in life when people celebrate.
How many can you think of?
Here is one occasion to start your list off - birthdays!

It's not

When Jesus grew up he made friends with two sisters. Their names were Mary and Martha. They lived with their brother Lazarus in a little village called Bethany, which was near Jerusalem.

Martha and Mary worked from dawn until dusk. They baked fresh bread each day. First they had to grind the corn, and then make the dough. Twice a day the sisters fetched water from the well. The water pots were heavy and made their shoulders ache. They swept the house, made milk into cheese and washed clothes in the stream. Then there was spinning, weaving and sewing to be done. They had to make sure there was enough olive oil in the lamp which lit the house and enough fuel for the fire on which food was cooked. There was always plenty to do!

One day Jesus and his disciples came to the sisters' home. Martha welcomed her guests and hurried to make a meal for them. Mary sat down at Jesus' feet and listened to everything he had to say to her.

'It's not fair,' Martha muttered under her breath, as she worked.

'She ought to be helping me. But what is she doing? Nothing! She's just sitting at Jesus' feet and I'm left to do everything. It really isn't fair!' she grumbled.

Martha got more and more upset until she could not stand it any longer.

'Don't you care that Mary has left me to do all the work?' she shouted at Jesus. 'Tell her to come and help me!'

But Jesus didn't say what Martha wanted him to. Instead he said gently, 'Martha, Martha, you are worried and troubled about housework, but Mary knows that at this moment it is more important to listen to my teaching.'

You will find the story of Mary and Martha in Luke 10 v38-42

MAKING BREAD, BUTTER AND CHEESE

Bread was a basic part of every meal and it was baked each day. Salt and water were added to form dough which was kneaded into small loaves.

The dough was either cooked straight away for unleavened or flat bread or left to rise before it was cooked for leavened bread.

There were two kinds of simple oven. One was an earthenware or metal plate supported by stones and placed over a fire. The other looked rather like a chimney. The fire was lit at the bottom and bread, resembling pancakes, was stuck to the sides of the chimney.

Women also had to make their own butter and cheese. A bag containing goat's milk was hung from three sticks. The women punched the bag from side to side until the milk turned to butter.

To make cheese, goat's milk was mixed with salt until it thickened, and then left to harden in the sun.

fair!

THE GOOD NEWS IS ...
Martha was too busy to listen to Jesus. But Jesus wants us to stop rushing around and spend some time quietly listening to him today.

WOMEN

A Jewish male would pray these words, "Thank you, God, that I am not a woman." Women were not thought to be as important as men. But in Luke's gospel there are many stories about women which show that Jesus considered women to be important.

WATER

Women fetched water twice a day from the well. Water was drawn in a leather bucket on a piece of rope. There was usually a long tiring walk home with a water jar balanced on the shoulder or head.

MEALS

A light breakfast of bread, fruit and cheese was eaten, but the main meals were at midday and in the evening. Figs, pomegranates, dates and mulberries were popular fruits.

Onions, beans, lentils, leeks and garlic were boiled or stewed. Small cucumbers were eaten raw.

Fish was often eaten, but meat was a luxury eaten on special occasions. There were very strict rules about how meat should be prepared.

Poor people normally sat on the floor to eat. At a dinner party there would be a seating plan showing the importance of each guest. Guests would lie on low couches or mats and eat with their fingers.

DID YOU KNOW?

Locusts and grasshoppers were eaten in Bible times and were considered to be a delicacy! They were often served with honey.

LISTEN AND LEARN

Mary realised it was important to listen to Jesus and learn from him.

Do you spend any of your time with Jesus? See if you can spend a few minutes each day reading your Bible, praying and listening to Jesus. See if you can buy some children's Bible Study notes to help you understand the Bible.

OH BROTHER!

Mary and Martha had a brother called Lazarus. Read the amazing story of how Jesus brought Lazarus back to life in **John 11 v1-44.**

A DAY'S WORK

Here is a list of some of Mary and Martha's tasks.
Compare how we would do the same things today.

Mary and Martha

Go to the well for water.
Grind corn into flour.
Make bread.
Milk the goat.
Sweep the floor.
Take clothes to the stream to wash.
Put oil in the lamp.

Today

Turn on the tap.
Buy bread in the supermarket.
(Now you finish the list!)
Aren't there a lot of things to be done!

HELPING HANDS

Although it is very important to spend time with Jesus, the housework has to be done too!
Think of ways you can help in your home.
Why not say thank you to the people who do things in your home by making them a fancy flowerpot!
You will need a clean clay flowerpot, some acrylic paints, a paintbrush and some newspaper.
1. Lay out your newspaper, so that you don't get paint everywhere!
2. Paint your flowerpot in stripes or spots or a bright pattern.
3. Let the paint dry.
4. You could then add some potting soil and a plant.
5. Add a ribbon and deliver your gift.

Perhaps you have an elderly neighbour you can help by offering to do some shopping or simple jobs in their house.

PLAYDOUGH

Mary and Martha worked hard to make fresh dough each day. But you could try making playdough. When you mix water, oil and flour you make dough. This is how you make playdough.
You will need -
10 heaped tablespoons of plain flour
8 tablespoons of warm water
4 teaspoons of oil
1 teaspoon of salt
A bowl

Mix the salt and flour in the bowl. Add the water a little bit at a time. Mix it together using your hand. Knead the dough until it holds together and is not too sticky. Use the playdough to make models.
Make a model of your home, your family or your pet.
If you want to keep your model, ask an adult to bake it in an oven. This will make it hard. Bake at 350°F, 180°C, Gas mark 7 for 30 minutes. The models will keep for a long time if they are really dried

WOMEN IN THE BIBLE

How much do you know about other women in the Bible? Test your knowledge!

1. Which woman prayed for a baby? Her prayer was answered when Samuel was born. Look in 1 Samuel 1 v12.
2. Which woman became a queen and saved God's people from being killed by the wicked Haman? Look in Esther 7 v1-6
3. Which woman showed great loyalty to her mother-in-law, Naomi, and to the God of Israel? Look in Ruth 1 v16.
4. Which old woman was a prophetess and realised that baby Jesus was God's own son? Look in Luke 2 v36-38.
5. Which woman was a prophet and judge of Israel? Look in Judges 4 v4.

Answers on page 64

NAPKIN RINGS

It seems Mary and Martha often welcomed Jesus into their home and he probably ate with them.

Why not make a set of napkin rings for your family or friends, so that the table looks lovely when they eat with you.

You will need a cardboard roll, (the inside of a toilet roll or kitchen roll will do), a pencil, glue, scissors, a ruler, some coloured felt and some braid.

1. Cut the roll into 3cm pieces.
2. Cover the roll with felt. Put some glue on the roll and roll it along the felt. Trim the edges.
3. Stick a piece of braid onto the felt for decoration or glue felt initials of your family onto the rings.

MAKE YOUR OWN FLOUR

Mary and Martha had to work hard to make flour every day. Buy some wheat from a health food shop. Look for two flattish stones. Put some wheat on one stone and grind the other stone on top of the wheat grains. After some hard work you will make flour!

A BUCKET OF WATER

Mary and Martha had to carry water home from the well.

Try carrying a bucket of water. It feels very heavy if you carry it a long way. Perhaps you could carry your bucket of water to the car and wash it.

PICTURE FRAME

Mary, Martha and Lazarus were brother and sisters. They were very fond of each other.

Make a picture frame and put a photograph of your brother or sister in it. Perhaps it will remind you to pray for them or do something kind for them each day.

You will need a strong piece of coloured card (you could paint a piece of stiff card), some ribbon, coloured elastic or braid, some light coloured card, glue, scissors and photograph.

1. Cut the strong coloured card 3cm larger than the photograph.
2. Cut the ribbon (braid or coloured elastic) into 4cm pieces and place them across each corner of the strong coloured card.
3. Stick the ends down on the back.
4. Cut out a piece of light card the same size as the strong card. Stick the light card over the back of the ribbon ends.
5. Cut a strip of light card 4cm wide. Fold down one end. Stick the folded end to the back of the frame to help it stand up.
6. Put your photograph under the ribbons.

(If you do not have a brother or sister, make the frame and use a photograph of someone you love.)

THE GOOD NEWS IS ... Jesus was able to forgive all the paralysed man's sins. Jesus can also forgive us for all the wrong things we have done.

Raise the

'He's back! Jesus is here!' shouted people, as they rushed through the narrow streets of Capernaum. Soon the house where Jesus was staying was so full that there wasn't room for one more person. There were people perched in the windows and the doorway was blocked. They all wanted to listen to Jesus teaching about God. Then four men arrived at the house, carrying a paralysed man. The men believed Jesus could heal their friend, but they couldn't get near Jesus because of the crowd. So they carried their friend up the stairs at the side of the house and onto the roof. Then they made a hole in the clay roof and let the man down through the opening. The people inside the house were astonished as the paralysed man appeared right in front of Jesus.

Jesus looked up at the four faces peering through the hole in the roof. He saw how much the men believed he would help, so he

HOUSEBUILDING

Ordinary people lived in simple houses that had only one room. The foundations were made of stone, but the walls were usually made of mud bricks dried in the sun. The walls were then plastered with mud. When it was wet these walls let water in. Windows were tiny and had no glass, so houses were often dark, even during the day. The floors were just mud or clay which was trodden down until it was hard. Insects crawled about the house in the hot summers and during the winter the room was filled with smoke from the fire. The houses of the rich were very different. Their houses might have as many as twelve rooms, built around a central courtyard.

INSIDE A HOUSE

The single room was divided into two parts.

At one end of the room was a raised platform where the family sat, slept and ate in bad weather. They would sit and sleep on mats placed on the floor. They slept in their working clothes and covered themselves with their cloaks or with goat's hair quilts. The women worked on the platform and kept their cooking utensils there. The farming tools and large storage jars of food and oil were kept on the lower level of the room. The animals' food troughs were also kept here and this is where the animals slept at night.

roof

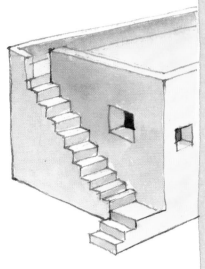

said to the paralysed man, 'Your sins are forgiven.'

Some of the Jewish leaders heard this and thought to themselves, 'Only God can forgive sins. Does he think he is God?'

Jesus knew what they were thinking and said, 'I'll prove to you who I am by healing this man.' Then he turned to the paralysed man and said, 'Pick up your mat and go home.' The man got up, picked up his mat and pushed his way through the crowd, praising God!

Everyone in the house was amazed and the paralysed man's four friends were delighted. They all praised God and said, 'We've never seen anything like this!'

Find this story in Mark 2 v1-12.

THE ROOF

The roofs of houses were flat. They were made of planks of wood covered with twigs or branches. A layer of clay was then added and made firm by using a stone roller. The roof was strong enough to walk on, although a hole could easily be made. There was usually a staircase going up the outside of the house leading to the roof. Poorer houses had a ladder. When it rained the roof often leaked and sometimes grass grew on the roof. Then the animals might be sent onto the roof to graze!

Flat roofs were used as a place to eat meals, to dry fruit and grain and to sleep on a warm night. The Law insisted that a low wall was built around the roof to stop people falling off it! (See Deuteronomy 22 v8.)

THE LAMP

The lamp was one of the most important items in a household. It was made by the potter, filled with olive oil and with a rag wick. The houses were very dark, so the lamp was kept alight at all times and placed on a shelf cut out of the wall.

DID YOU KNOW?

Houses were sometimes built so close together you could walk from roof top to roof top!

GET WELL SOON

You will need: two pieces of card, crayons/felt-tip pens, scissors and an envelope.

1. Fold one piece of card in half to make a greetings card.
2. Cut a slit near the top of the card.
3. Draw a body shape that will fit in the slit. Cut it out.
4. Put the body into the slit. Put measles on the face on the outside of the card.
5. Draw and colour some bedclothes on the front of the card with the 'measly' face sticking out of them.

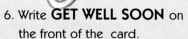
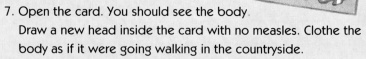

6. Write **GET WELL SOON** on the front of the card.
7. Open the card. You should see the body. Draw a new head inside the card with no measles. Clothe the body as if it were going walking in the countryside.
8. Can you visit someone who is poorly and give them the card? Or you could post it to them.

   If you do not know anyone who is ill, save it for another time.

AREAS OF MEDICINE

Medicine is a huge subject and doctors often become experts in a single area of medicine. The different areas of medicine have long and complicated names!

See if you can put these long and complicated words into the correct sentence.

   a) **Paediatrics**
   b) **Surgery**
   c) **Neurology**
   d) **Orthopaedics**
   e) **Ophthalmology**

1. The medical care of children is called ......
2. The care of bones and joints is called ......
3. Cutting into the body to cure illness is called ......
4. Looking after disorders of the brain and nerves is called ......
5. The treatment of eyes is called ......

   Have a guess!!
   Answers on page 64

HOMES

Start a collection of homes from around the world. Make a scrapbook of pictures. You will be amazed at the different types of homes! Some people live on boats, some houses are built on stilts, some homes are made of mud and some poor people live in cardboard boxes.

MY HOME

Living in a small home in the time of Jesus was not always very pleasant! Make a list of things you would not have liked about it. Now make a list of the things you like about your home.

Draw a picture of your home and say thank you to Jesus.

PICTURE IT!

Make a 2-D, moving picture to illustrate this story.
You will need two pieces of thin card (about 300mm by 210mm), a small piece of card, some glue, felt pens and some scissors.

1. Cut a door and a window into one piece of card.
2. Glue the piece of card with the door in it around the edge and stick it onto the other piece of card the same size. BUT leave a gap that has no glue. See the diagram.
3. On the small piece of card draw the paralysed man. Attach a strip of card to one side of the man.

4. Draw Jesus inside the door of the house and draw other people in the crowd outside and inside the house.
5. Put the man on the mat through the gap in the roof and lower him down to Jesus.

A LAMP

The lamp was very important in a house in the time of Jesus.

Make a model of one using plasticine.

THINK ABOUT IT

The paralysed man in the story was unable to work, so he had to beg in order to live. If you were paralysed and could not use your hands, arms or legs what would you miss being able to do?

Look at your town. What would it be difficult for a person in a wheelchair to do?

HELP!

Is there any way you can help a charity to help sick or paralysed people?

SAY A PRAYER

Doctors can do wonderful things to make people better, but Jesus still wants us to pray for people who are ill. This is because Jesus can still help people to get well! Pray for somebody you know who is unwell.

READ ALL ABOUT IT

There are lots of stories in the Bible that tell about Jesus healing people. Read one of them in **Luke 5 v12-16.** Did you know that Luke who wrote down this story was a doctor?

Tax, a tree

Zacchaeus was a small man with a big name and an important job. He was the chief tax collector in Jericho, and this made him very rich, because he kept a lot of the money for himself. One day Jesus was passing through Jericho and Zacchaeus wanted to see him. He was not the only one! A big crowd had gathered along the road and Zacchaeus was too short to see over everyone. So, although he was an important man, he decided to climb a sycomore tree and watch from there. When Jesus came by he looked up at Zacchaeus and called him by name! 'Zacchaeus! Come down quickly. I am going to be a guest in your home today.'

TAX COLLECTORS

In the time of Jesus, some Jews had the job of collecting taxes for the Romans. This money was used to pay for the Roman government. Most Jews hated the tax collectors, because they worked for the conquering Romans and they were often dishonest. They took more money than was due and they kept the extra for themselves!

MONEY

The Romans made their coins out of gold or silver. The Jews had to use bronze or copper. Roman coins often had the head of the emperor on them. Jewish coins had pictures of plants or other symbols. This Jewish coin shows a Menorah (seven-branched candlestick) and it was probably made in a mould. Roman coins had to be used to pay the tax collector.

THE SYCOMORE TREE

The sycomore tree is a type of fig tree. It is a different tree from the European sycamore tree or the North American plane, also called sycamore. It grows to be about twelve metres high, has widely spreading branches and ever-green leaves. It can still be seen on the streets of some towns in Israel.

and tea

Zacchaeus scrambled down.

The people in the crowd were cross and began to complain and grumble. 'He has gone to be the guest of a wicked man,' they muttered. But Zacchaeus said to Jesus, 'I will give half of everything I own to the poor, and anyone I've cheated I will pay them back four times as much.'

Jesus replied, 'I have come to find and save people like you, Zacchaeus.' Then Jesus and Zacchaeus continued on their way to Zacchaeus' house.

Find this story in the Bible in Luke 19 v1-10.

MEALS

Eating a meal was an important event in the first century. There were rules about what you should eat and where people could sit at the table! There were even rules about who you should eat with. Some kinds of people, like tax collectors, were not thought to be suitable company.

Eating together was a sign of friendship. So the Jews were shocked and surprised when Jesus went to be the guest of Zacchaeus. Not only was Jesus breaking the rules, they realised he was offering to be Zacchaeus' friend and they strongly disapproved.

DID YOU KNOW ?

Zacchaeus was a popular Puritan name in 17th century England?

Do you know anyone called Zacchaeus today?

THE GOOD NEWS IS... Jesus loves everyone no matter who they are or what they have done! Even if we have no other friends Jesus is our friend!

THE CLIMBING COLLECTOR

You will need: scissors, thin card, coloured crayons / felt pens, sticky tape and string.

1. Draw a tree on the card and make two holes as shown.
2. Colour it. Cut it out.
3. Draw Zacchaeus and make two holes as shown.
4. Colour him and cut him out.
5. Thread a piece of string through the holes in Zacchaeus and the tree as shown. Tie the string in a knot at the back of the tree.
6. Fasten the string to the back of Zacchaeus with sticky tape.
7. Pull the string to make Zacchaeus go up and down.

CRAYONS AND COINS

You will need: wax crayons, paper and coins

1. Put the coin under a piece of paper.
2. Rub over the top of the coin with the wax crayon.
3. See if you can create a picture or write a word in this way, eg. make a tree.

COIN COLLECTION

Start a collection of foreign coins.

SAD TO SAVED

Zacchaeus was a very unhappy man, even though he owned a lot of money. When he met Jesus and saw how much Jesus loved him, Zacchaeus wanted to change, so he gave all his money away. That not only made him happy, but a lot of others too. Can you design a sad to happy face that changes when it is turned around?

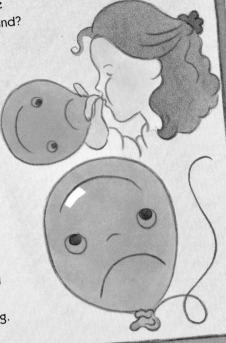

You will need: a balloon, a permanent marker pen and string.

1. Blow the balloon up.
2. Draw a face as shown on the balloon with the pen.
3. Turn the balloon around and see a sad face change to a happy face. Attach the string.

IT MAKES YOU THINK...

Do you know anyone who is lonely and needs a friend? Think about how you can help them.

See if you can help a person to have a happy face and not a sad face.

PRESS A PICTURE

You will need: blotting paper, some heavy books, a large piece of paper and glue.

1. Collect and name as many different leaves from trees as you can.
2. Place the leaves between the blotting paper and put them under some heavy books. This will press them.
3. Make a chart. Stick one of each kind of leaf on a large piece of paper and write its name under it.
4. Make a picture using leaves stuck onto a contrasting colour background.

WORKING WITH OUTCASTS

Jesus spent time with people no one else cared about like the tax collectors.
Can you find out about two people that have followed Jesus' example?

READ ALL ABOUT IT

Jesus made another tax collector one of his disciples. Read about it in the Bible.
Luke 5 v27-31

Not a bite

THE FISHERMAN'S JOB

It was hard work being a fisherman. Fishing took place at night and during the day the fish were cleaned, sorted and sold. When the fish were sorted they were put into baskets ready to be taken to market. They were normally salted to stop them from going bad. The nets also had to be cleaned and repaired. Then they were hung up to dry.

The work was not only tiring, it was often dangerous. The Sea of Galilee was well known for its sudden storms. Jesus and his disciples were caught in one of these storms and even the experienced fishermen were frightened. Read about it in Luke 8 v22-25

After Jesus rose from the dead, the disciples saw him less often. They were not certain what Jesus wanted them to do next, so they waited for his instructions.

'I'm going fishing,' announced Peter one night to James and John and four other disciples.

'We'll go with you,' they replied. So the seven men pushed the boat out into the deep water of the Sea of Galilee and let down their nets. They fished all night, but they didn't catch anything. They felt tired, cold and disappointed because they had no fish to show for all their hard work.

As the sun was rising they sailed back to the shore. There was a man standing at the water's edge. He shouted to the fishermen,

'Have you caught anything?'

'Nothing,' they answered.

THE BOATS

A fisherman's boat was quite small and held only about six men. It had a single sail or could be propelled by oars. Sometimes fishermen worked together as partners and clubbed together to buy a boat.

all night

'Throw your net out on the right side of your boat and you will catch plenty,' said the man.

Although the disciples were tired they did as the stranger said and threw their net out. The net filled with fish and the men could hardly pull it in! Then the disciples realised the man on the shore was Jesus! Peter was so excited that he jumped into the water and waded back to the beach. The other men came to shore in the boat. Peter helped them drag the net full of big fish ashore and they counted them. There were one hundred and fifty-three!

Jesus had made a charcoal fire and grilled some fish on it.

'Come and eat,' invited Jesus. The fishermen gladly warmed themselves by the fire and ate bread and fish for breakfast as they talked to Jesus.

Find this story in John 21 v1-14

METHODS OF FISHING

The Israelites knew very little about fishing in Old Testament times. They only had one word for 'fish' in their language. This word was used to describe the smallest tiddler and the big fish that swallowed Jonah!

By New Testament times fishing was more important. There were four main ways of catching fish.

a. A light was shone on the water from a boat and the fish were speared.

b. A bone hook was fitted to the end of a line and it was trailed in the water from the boat.

c. A small round net was thrown into the water by a fisherman standing on the shore or in the shallow water. Weights on the edge made it sink and the fish were taken by surprise and caught in it. The net was pulled back to shore.

d. A large net about 500 metres long was stretched out between two boats. The net closed around the fish and trapped them. The net was then dragged aboard. This was the best way to catch a lot of fish.

DID YOU KNOW THAT?
There were fourteen kinds of fish in the Sea of Galilee.

THE GOOD NEWS IS ... Jesus was interested in the disciples' everyday life as fishermen. He cares about the things we do every day too.

SEA MUSIC

Jesus and his disciples spent a lot of their time on or near the Sea of Galilee.

Listen to some music about the sea, such as Bizet's "The Pearl Fishers" or "La Mer" by Debussy.

A FISHY PICNIC

Jesus and his disciples had barbecued fish and bread for breakfast on the beach.

Go on a picnic with your friends or family and take fish sandwiches. Think of Jesus and the picnic he had with his friends.

THE LORD GOD MADE THEM ALL

God made hundreds of types of fish. There were fourteen types of fish in the Sea of Galilee, but there are many more types of fish in the world. See how many you can name.

Go and visit an aquarium and enjoy the wonderful colour and shapes of tropical fish.

COLLAGE

Make a picture of the shore by the Sea of Galilee when the disciples met Jesus that morning as the sun was rising.

Use materials such as sandpaper for the sand, torn-up pieces of blue paper from magazines for the sea, and small twigs and red sweet papers for the fire.

CATCH A FISH

The disciples had empty nets until Jesus helped them to catch some fish. See if you can put a fish in an empty net.

You will need two 7cm squares of paper, a pencil and some sellotape.

1. Draw an empty net on one piece of paper and a fish on the other.
2. Sellotape the squares together, inserting the pencil between them.
3. Roll the pencil between your hands so that the fish appears in the net.

CRAB PLATES

Make crab plates for your fishy picnic.
You will need an orange coloured paper plate (white would do), some orange paper, some glue and a black felt pen.

1. Draw two eyes on the plate.
2. Cut out 8 legs. Fold them and stick them to the underside of the plate.
3. Cut out 2 pincers and stick them to the underside of the plate.

FISHERS OF MEN

When Jesus first met his disciples who were fishermen he told them, 'I will make you fishers of men.' Jesus meant they would not be catching fish for a living any more, but telling people about Jesus. They would be 'catching' followers for Jesus!
Say a prayer for some of the people you know who are not Christians, that they might become friends of Jesus. You could write their name on a fish shape to remind you to pray for them.

A FISHY QUIZ

Look up the Bible references to find the answers to these fishy questions.

1. What did Jesus use to feed 5,000 people?
   Find out in Luke 9 v13.
2. What was Jonah swallowed by when he tried to disobey God?
   Find out in Jonah 1 v17.
3. Where did Peter find a coin?
   Find out in Matthew 17 v27.
4. What did Jesus have to eat when he appeared to his disciples after having risen from the dead?
   Find out in Luke 24 v41-43.

Answers on page 64

HOVERCRAFT

Peter and the other disciples knew nothing about hovercrafts!
A hovercraft is a quick way to travel across water today.
See if you can make this toy hovercraft.
You will need a polystyrene food tray, a cork, a balloon, plasticine, a knitting needle, a pencil and some glue.

1. Ask an adult to make a hole through the cork with the knitting needle.
2. Make a hole in the food tray with the pencil. Stick the cork over the tray, so that the holes are lined up.
3. Put plasticine around the hole to stop any air escaping. You will need a smooth surface. Blow up the balloon and fit it over the cork. Try not to let any air escape.
4. Push the tray gently and watch it glide away.

A new

S aul the Pharisee hated the followers of Jesus. He had them put in prison, beaten and even put to death. He thought he was doing what God wanted him to do. Some of the followers of Jesus escaped to the city of Damascus, so Saul followed them. He wanted to bring them back to Jerusalem as prisoners.

Saul and his men were travelling along the road to Damascus in the hot sun, when suddenly a bright light shone down on Saul. He was blinded and fell to the ground.

'Saul! Saul! Why are you persecuting me?' said a voice from heaven.

'Who is speaking?' replied Saul nervously.

'I am Jesus whom you are persecuting. Get up and go to Damascus and you will be told what to do,' the voice answered.

The men with Saul led him into the city. After three days God restored Saul's sight and he was baptised as a Christian. Saul's life was completed changed. Now he began to teach others that Jesus

TRAVEL

Paul went on three long missionary journeys to take the good news of Jesus to countries around the Mediterranean Sea. In those days travelling was difficult and dangerous. Like most people, Paul and his helpers travelled on foot. Rich people could hire horse-drawn chariots. Asses, mules, camels and horses were also used. The Romans built good roads and throughout their empire travel became easier.

Sea travel was risky and it was only safe to cross the Mediterranean Sea in summer. Paul usually sailed in Roman ships, but he was shipwrecked on a winter voyage to Rome.

DID YOU KNOW?

Paul wrote thirteen of the twenty-seven New Testament books.

PERSECUTION

The number of followers of Jesus grew quickly after his death and resurrection. Many Jews began to follow Jesus and this made the Jewish leaders angry and jealous. Many followers of Jesus were arrested and beaten.

The name Christian was first given to followers of Jesus as a nickname. Because Christians refused to worship the Roman emperor many were imprisoned and put to death. It was three hundred years before the Romans allowed Christians to worship freely.

life

was the Son of God. He changed his name to Paul and began to travel with helpers to other countries to tell people about Jesus. Soon there were groups of believers in many towns. Paul wrote letters to them teaching them about their new faith.

In Paul's letter to his friend Timothy he wrote that life is like a race. Just as athletes in a race have to keep the rules, so Christians need to obey God's rules.

Paul's life was full of adventure but he also suffered as a follower of Jesus. Eventually his enemies had him arrested and imprisoned in Rome. When Paul knew he hadn't long to live he wrote, 'I have done my best in the race, I have run the full distance, and I have kept the faith. And now there is waiting for me the victory prize which God will give me.'

Find the story of how Paul became a follower of Jesus in Acts 9 v1-22.

THE PHARISEES

Saul was brought up as a Pharisee. The Pharisees were Jews who studied every detail of God's commandments and laws to his people. They also added many other laws of their own, which people had to obey too. Some of the Pharisees thought Jesus was a good man, but many of them were jealous of him.

SPORT

Paul mentioned sport in many of his letters. The athletic contests he mentions were Greek Games, like our Olympic Games. Greek boys trained in running, wrestling, boxing, javelin, discus and long jump. Training was long and hard. Runners trained with weights tied to their bodies. The weights were taken off just before the race, so that it seemed easy to run. The rules were strict and anyone who broke the rules was beaten.

Greek games were held in important cities. Many towns would send teams to compete. All the competitors were naked. The winners were presented with crowns of pine, laurel or olive leaves and were greatly honoured.

HELLO

Paul travelled to many countries to tell them about Jesus. People still travel as missionaries to other countries to teach others about Jesus.

Learn to say good morning and goodbye in some other languages.

FRENCH
Bonjour
Au revoir

ITALIAN
Buon giorno
Arrivederci

GERMAN
Guten Morgen
Auf wiedersehen

ENGLISH
Good morning
Goodbye

SPANISH
Buenas dias
Adios

GOOD NEWS FOR ALL

An evangelist is someone who preaches the good news of Jesus.

Billy Graham is a famous American evangelist. He became a Christian in 1934 when he was 16 years old. He has preached the gospel all over the world, often at huge rallies. Thousands of people have become Christians through listening to him.

There have been many Christians from the time of Jesus until now who have been involved in helping others to know Jesus. Some have become famous, like Paul, and you can read about them in books. Others are not famous, but they have told their friends and neighbours about Christ.

Do you have a friend or neighbour that you can tell about Jesus' love for them?

ALL CHANGE!

Saul changed completely when he met Jesus. He stopped persecuting Christians and started preaching about Jesus! He even changed his name.

There are a number of changes that take place in nature. Can you match the pairs?

1. tadpole
2. caterpillar
3. acorn
4. apple pip

a. oak tree
b. frog
c. apple tree
d. butterfly

Answers on page 64

KEEP FIT

All top sportsmen and women have to keep fit. They train hard each day.

Try to do some running, jumping, squat thrusts, swimming or a team sport to keep fit.

Paul wrote that you need to 'keep fit' as a Christian too. You can do this by reading your Bible, praying, reading Christian books and meeting with other Christians.

TEAMWORK

How many team sports can you name?

Paul always travelled with friends and they worked as a team. Here are some of his friends' names - Barnabas, Mark, Silas, Luke and Timothy. It isn't always easy being in a team and working with others. You have to learn to be unselfish, let others do things you want to do, be patient and listen to other people's ideas. Paul and his team sometimes argued!

But Paul knew God wants Christians to work together. **Read what Paul wrote to the Corinthians in 1 Corinthians 12 v12-27.**

A SECRET SIGN

In sport, teams wear different kits so the players and spectators know who is on which team. Why don't you design a football strip or an outfit for another team game?

The early Christians were persecuted and sometimes killed for being followers of Jesus. They had s secret sign - the fish - to show they were Christians. Other followers of Jesus knew that the fish sign meant they were on 'God's team'.

The Greek word for fish was **ICTHUS.** The letters in this word formed the first letters of the sentence **'Iesous Christos THeou Uios Soter'** which means 'Jesus Christ Son of God and Saviour'.

Make a fish badge using a circle of card, some sellotape and a safety pin.

Look out for the sign of the fish. Christians still display it today.

A FLICK BOOK

Paul often wrote about running in his letters.
See if you can draw a running man.
You will need a small notebook (or some pieces of paper stapled together) and a black pen.

In the bottom right hand corner of each page of the notebook draw a stick man running.
Start with him standing still, the next picture he begins to move, in the next picture his legs and arms move a little more and so on.

When you have used each page, flick the corner of the book and watch your stick men run.

PAUL'S LETTERS

Using the contents page of your New Testament see if you can unscramble the following names of Paul's letters.

1. NSPPPAILIHPI
2. RONTHINAICS
3. MARONS
4. OLCSSSNSIAO
5. TUTSI

Answers on page 64

BE A SPECTATOR

Athletics has always been popular. The inspiration for the Olympic Games came from the Greek Games held over 2000 years ago. The Olympic Games are held every 4 years. Over 120 countries send athletes to compete in more than 20 different sports. More than 7000 sportsmen and women take part. There is no prize money, just medals for the winners.

See if you can go and watch some athletes competing. If not, there is often athletics on TV.

In order to win a race an athlete must fix his/her eyes on the finishing line and run straight towards it. An athlete can't stop for a rest in the race or give up or look at what other people are doing.

In the Christian race of life we need to keep trying and fix our eyes on Jesus (read Hebrews 12 v1-2).

Make yourself a gold medal to remind yourself of this.
You will need some ribbon, a circle of yellow card and a pen.
Thread the ribbon through the card and write on your medal

FIX YOUR EYES ON JESUS.

OLD TESTAMENT MAP

Map of Palestine showing the location of the Old Testament stories shown in this book.

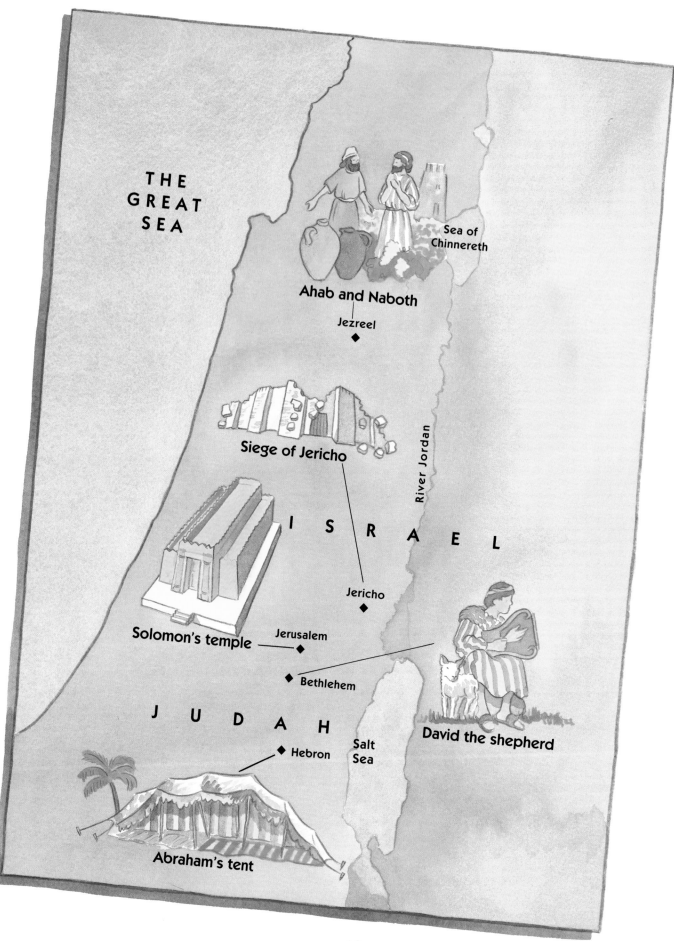

THE
GREAT
SEA

Sea of
Chinnereth

Ahab and Naboth

Jezreel

Siege of Jericho

River Jordan

I S R A E L

Jericho

Solomon's temple

Jerusalem

Bethlehem

David the shepherd

J U D A H

Salt
Sea

Hebron

Abraham's tent

NEW TESTAMENT MAP

Map of Palestine showing the location of the New Testament stories shown in this book.

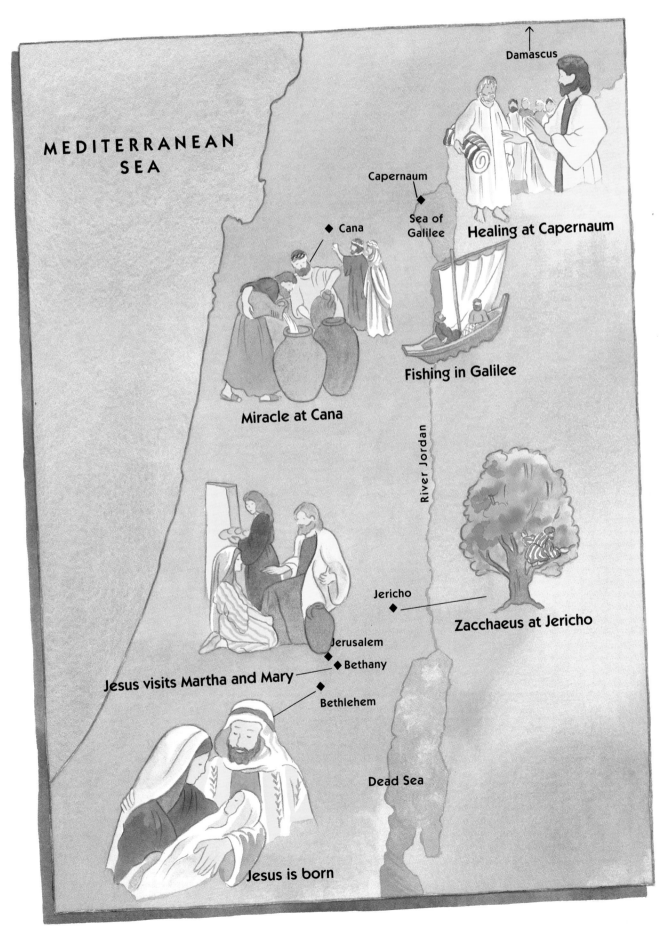

MEDITERRANEAN SEA

Damascus

Capernaum

Sea of Galilee

Cana

Healing at Capernaum

Fishing in Galilee

Miracle at Cana

River Jordan

Jericho

Zacchaeus at Jericho

Jerusalem

Bethany

Jesus visits Martha and Mary

Bethlehem

Dead Sea

Jesus is born

ANSWERS FOR ACTIVITY PAGES

P12-13
KNOW YOUR NAME: Lincoln
SAND AND STARS: 11 stars

P16-17
JERICHO STORIES: Luke 19 v1-10
FAMOUS WALLS: 1-d. 2-b. 3-a. 4-c.
7 SUMS: 1-84 2-66 3-81 4-15 5-35 6-40 7-7.

P20-21
SHEEP FACTS: All true!
A SHEPHERD'S STAFF: A bishop. A bishop takes care of and guides a flock of people!

P24-25
CAPITAL CITIES: 1-c. 2-e. 3-d. 4-b. 5-a.

P28-29
FAMOUS BUILDINGS: 1-b. 2-c. 3-d. 4-e. 5-a.
Notre Dame Cathedral is a place of worship.
RULERS AND LEADERS: 1-b 2-c 3-d 4-a
LOGS: 1. Boom men
2. To make paper
3. Count the rings inside the trunk. There is a ring for each year.

P32-33
MATCH THE PAIRS: 1-d 2-a 3-b 4-c

P36-37
JOHN THE BAPTIST: 1. River Jordan
2. Locusts and wild honey
3. To show they were sorry for their sins
4. A dove descended and God spoke
5. He was beheaded
A ROMAN CENSUS: August. From Julius Caesar comes the name July.

P40-41
MATCH THE PAIR: a-g b-i c-f d-h e-j

P44-45
WOMEN IN THE BIBLE:
1. Hannah
2. Esther
3. Ruth
4. Anna
5. Deborah

P48-49
AREAS OF MEDICINE: 1-a 2-d 3-b 4-c 5-e

P56-57
A FISHY QUIZ:
1. Five loaves and two fish
2. A large fish
3. In the mouth of a fish
4. A piece of cooked fish

P60-61
ALL CHANGE: 1-b 2-d 3-a 4-c
PAUL'S LETTERS:
1. Philippians
2. Corinthians
3. Romans
4. Colossians
5. Titus

INDEX